Barbara Wharram

Elementary Rudiments of Music

Revised Edition

edited by

Kathleen Wood

Library and Archives Canada Cataloguing in Publication

Wharram, Barbara
    Elementary rudiments of music / Barbara Wharram; edited by Kathleen Wood. —
Rev. ed.

ISBN 1-55440-011-2

    1. Music theory-Elementary works. 2. Music theory-Elementary
works-Problems, exercises, etc. I. Title.

MT7.W55 2005   781   C2005-903190-5

FREDERICK
HARRIS
MUSIC

ISBN 1-55440-011-2

Preface to the Original Edition, 1969

My sincere thanks for their criticism and advice go to several members of the teaching staff of the Royal Conservatory of Music of Toronto, especially Catherine Palmer, Margaret Parsons, and Clifford Poole, and also to the Principal Dr. David Ouchterlony, for their help and encouragement. Their assistance has been invaluable.

Throughout this book, the letter **P** before a paragraph number means that the paragraph contains material relevant to Preliminary Rudiments. A paragraph marked **1** applies to Grade One Rudiments, and a paragraph marked **2**, to Grade Two Rudiments. Paragraphs that are marked Optional are not required for examination purposes, but contain additional information that may be helpful to the student.

Barbara Wharram

To my daughters, Heather and Pam, and my grandsons, Sean, Adam, Matt, and Kyle.

Preface to the Revised Edition, 2005

Elementary Rudiments of Music has been a well-loved and well-used staple of music students for almost forty years. In that time, although the book has received numerous printings and small corrections, no major changes were needed. With the revisions to The Royal Conservatory of Music *Theory Syllabus* in 2002, a revised and expanded edition became necessary. The essential character of Barbara Wharram's book remains intact: however, new material and an updated approach to language lend this new edition a freshness and relevance that should appeal to a wide range of theory students of all ages.

Topics in theory are often interrelated. Therefore, the teacher and student are not expected to study one chapter after another from beginning to end. Use the designations of **P**, **1**, and **2** as a guide to assist you in charting a logical course of study.

Kathleen Wood

P is equivalent to…	Preliminary Rudiments/Basic Rudiments
1 is equivalent to…	Grade One Rudiments/Intermediate Rudiments
2 is equivalent to…	Grade Two Rudiments/Advanced Rudiments

CONTENTS

CHAPTER 1

NOTATION

THE MUSIC STAFF

P 1 2 1. A NOTE is the name given to a sign that is used to represent a musical sound. It is written on a set of parallel lines called a STAFF.

P 1 2 2. These lines, and the spaces between them, are given the names of the first seven letters of the alphabet, A B C D E F G.

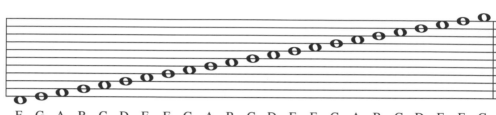

F G A B C D E F G A B C D E F G A B C D E F G

This many lines are difficult to read, and some of the lines are completely unnecessary for the different voices. Middle C can be used by every voice, so the lines are divided into two sets of five, leaving MIDDLE C between them, shown on a short line only when it is needed.

F G A B C D E F G A B C D E F G A B C D E F G

P 1 2 3. By the position of a note on this staff, you can tell its PITCH—that is, how high or how low its sound is. The higher up the note is on the staff, the higher its pitch will be, and the lower down on the staff, the lower its pitch will be.

P 1 2 4. A CLEF (from the French word "clé," meaning key) is a sign placed at the beginning of each staff, which tells you the exact pitch of one particular line. Since the names of the notes are in alphabetical order, if we are given the name of one line, we can easily name the notes on all the other lines and spaces of that clef.

P 1 2 5. The most commonly used clefs are the TREBLE or G clef and the BASS or F clef.

G   F

As you can see, the treble clef (which was originally written as a fancy capital G) curls around line 2, which fixes this line as the G above middle C. The bass clef (from an old form of the letter F) has two dots—one above and one below line 4, fixing this line as the F below middle C. Therefore, the notes in the treble and bass clefs are:

E G B D F   F A C E   G B D F A   A C E G

2 6.   Besides the treble and bass clefs, there used to be many others. Only one of these clefs now remains. This is called the C clef—🎼—and it fixes the place of middle C.

middle C

When it is placed on line 3, it is called the ALTO clef, and is used in music written for viola and alto trombone.

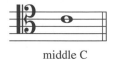

middle C

When it is placed on line 4, it is called the TENOR clef and is used in music written for the tenor trombone. The tenor clef is sometimes used for the upper range of the cello.

The notes in the ALTO clef are:
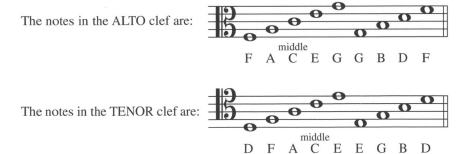

F A C E G G B D F

middle

The notes in the TENOR clef are:

D F A C E E G B D

middle

This illustration shows the relative position of the four clefs on the staff.

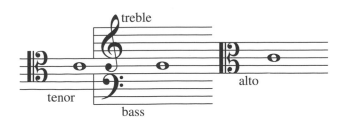

treble

tenor

bass

alto

P 1 2 7. If you want to write notes that are higher or lower than will fit on the staff, you can extend the staff by adding LEDGER LINES.

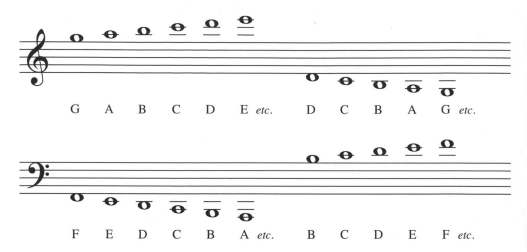

P 1 2 8. When putting STEMS on notes, be careful that you face them in the correct direction. For music with a single musical part in each staff, all the notes above the middle line should have their stems going down, and all the notes below the middle line should have their stems going up. The stem of a note on the third line can go up or down, but down is preferred.

These are all correct:

But these are not:

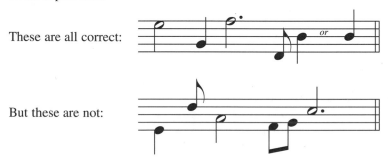

When a group of notes is joined by a BEAM, the direction of the stems depends on which note is farthest away from the middle line—the highest one or the lowest one.

Here, E is farther away from B than C is, so all the stems go up:

Here, E is farther away from B than G is, so all the stems go down:

P 1 2   EXERCISES

1.   Write the following notes in the treble clef.

a) F on a line   f) F in a space
b) A in a space   g) B on a line
c) G on a line   h) D in a space
d) C in a space   i) G in a space
e) E on a line   j) middle C

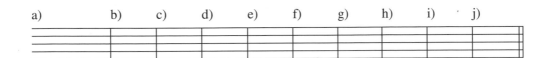

2.   Write the following notes in the bass clef.

a) B in a space   f) D on a line
b) F on a line   g) G in a space
c) middle C   h) F in a space
d) A on a line   i) G on a line
e) E in a space   j) C in a space

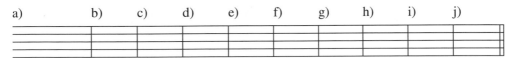

3.   Name each of the following notes.

4.   Name each of the following notes.

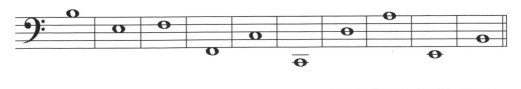

5.   Name each of the following notes.

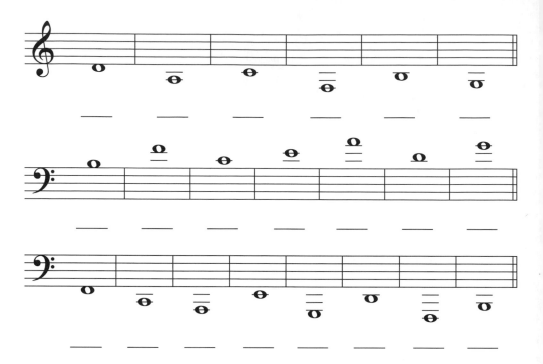

NOTE: If you need more experience in naming notes, practice on a separate sheet of staff paper.

2   MORE EXERCISES

1.   Name each of the following notes.

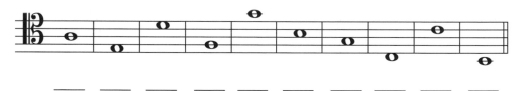

2.   Name each of the following notes.

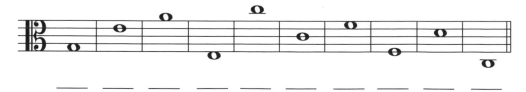

3. Write the following notes in the alto clef.

a) A on a line   f) B in a space
b) G on a line   g) A in a space
c) D in a space   h) middle C
d) F on a line   i) G in a space
e) E in a space   j) E on a line

a)   b)   c)   d)   e)   f)   g)   h)   i)   j)

4. Write the following notes in the tenor clef.

a) D on a line   f) F on a line
b) G in a space   g) middle C
c) A on a line   h) F in a space
d) E in a space   i) B in a space
e) D in a space   j) E on a line

a)   b)   c)   d)   e)   f)   g)   h)   i)   j)

TIME VALUES

P 1 2   9. The lengths (or durations) of sounds are written as NOTES of different shapes. The lengths (or durations) of periods of silence are written as RESTS of different shapes. Here is a chart showing the different kinds of notes and their corresponding rests.

breve note	𝄚𝅝𝄚	▪	breve rest
whole note	𝅝	▬	whole rest
half note	𝅗𝅥	▬	half rest
quarter note	𝅘𝅥	𝄽	quarter rest
eighth note	𝅘𝅥𝅮	𝄾	eighth rest
sixteenth note	𝅘𝅥𝅯	𝄿	sixteenth rest
thirty-second note	𝅘𝅥𝅰	𝅀	thirty-second rest

The relative time values of the above notes are:

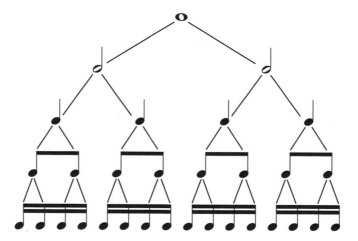

The relative time values portion shows:

Each note or rest in the chart has twice the value of the next one down, as shown in the following graph:

P 1 2   10.   For music with a single musical part on the staff, rests are placed as follows:

P 1 2 11. A DOT placed after a note or rest increases the length by one-half of its original value. Thus,

$$\text{𝅗𝅥. } = \text{𝅗𝅥} + \text{𝅘𝅥}$$

$$\text{𝅘𝅥. } = \text{𝅘𝅥} + \text{𝅘𝅥𝅮}$$

$$\text{𝅘𝅥𝅮. } = \text{𝅘𝅥𝅮} + \text{𝅘𝅥𝅯}$$

$$\text{𝄾. } = \text{𝄾} + \text{𝄿}$$

A second dot increases the length by one-half of the value of the first dot. Thus,

$$\text{𝅗𝅥.. } = \text{𝅗𝅥} + \text{𝅘𝅥} + \text{𝅘𝅥𝅮}$$

$$\text{𝅘𝅥.. } = \text{𝅘𝅥} + \text{𝅘𝅥𝅮} + \text{𝅘𝅥𝅯}$$

$$\text{𝄿.. } = \text{𝄿} + \text{𝅀} + \text{𝅁}$$

P 1 2 12. For music with a single musical part in each staff, dots are placed as follows:

For a note in a space, the dot goes in the same space:

For a note on a line, the dot goes in the space above:

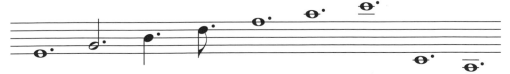

For rests, dots go in the third space of the staff:

P 1 2   13.   Another way of increasing the time value of a note is to use a TIE. This is a curved line joining two notes of the same pitch. It indicates that the second note is not to be sounded, but that the first note is to be held for the combined duration of both.

When a curved line is placed over notes of different pitch, it is known as a SLUR. Do not confuse the tie and the slur. (For more about slurs, see Chapter 10, paragraph 18, pp. 262–263.)

P 1 2   EXERCISES

1.   Write *one* note that is equal to the value of each of the following.

a)  =

d) =

b) =

e) =

c) =

f) =

2.   Write *one* rest that is equal to the value of each of the following.

a) =

f) =

b) =

g) =

c) =

h) =

d) =

i) =

e) =

j) =

3.   Write *three* notes that are equal to the value of each of the following.

a) =

c) =

b) =

d) =

4. Write *two* rests that are equal to the value of each of the following.

   a) 𝄽   =   c) 𝄾   =

   b) ▬   =   d) 𝄽· =

5. Complete the following statements.

   a) 2 quarter notes   = _____ eighth notes
   b) 1 half note   = _____ quarter notes
   c) 3 eighth notes   = _____ sixteenth notes
   d) 1 quarter note   = _____ sixteenth notes
   e) 2 eighth notes   = _____ quarter note
   f) 4 sixteenth notes   = _____ eighth notes
   g) 2 half notes   = _____ whole note
   h) 1 whole note   = _____ eighth notes
   i) 4 thirty-second notes = _____ sixteenth notes
   j) 2 sixteenth notes   = _____ eighth note
   k) 1 dotted quarter note = _____ eighth notes
   l) 3 half notes   = _____ whole notes
   m) 4 half notes   = _____ breve note
   n) 6 sixteenth notes   = _____ thirty-second notes
   o) 1 dotted half note   = _____ quarter notes

6. Write a single note (or a dotted note) which is equal to the value of each of the
    following.

   a)    f)

   b)    g)

   c)    h)

   d)    i)

   e)    j)

14

7. Write a single rest (or dotted rest) which is equal to the value of each of the following.

a) ♪ ♪ ♪ =   e) ▬ ▬ =

b) ▬ ▬ =   f) 𝄾 ♪ ♪ =

c) 𝄾 ♪ =   g) ▬ ▬ =

d) ♪ ♪ ♪ =   h) ♪ ♪ ♪ =

8. Write a single note (or dotted note) which is equal to the value of each of the following.

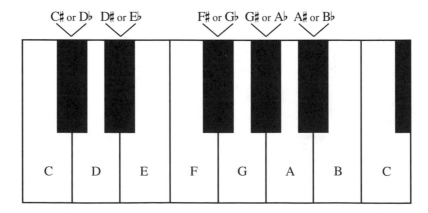

TONES, SEMITONES, AND ACCIDENTALS

P 1 2 14. A SEMITONE is the smallest distance between two sounds used in Western art music, and the smallest distance between any two adjacent keys on the piano, whether black and white, or white and white—that is, the distance from one key to the next key with no key between.

C to C♯ (or D♭) is a semitone. D♯ (or E♭) to E is a semitone. But also note that there is a semitone between E and F, since there is no black key between these notes.

P 1 2   15.   A TONE (or WHOLE TONE) is equal to two semitones in succession, in the same direction. C to D is a tone, F♯ to G♯ is a tone, E to F♯ is a tone, and so on.

As you can see, the black notes have no names of their own, and have to borrow from one of the white notes nearest to them. For example, the black note between C and D, if it borrows from C, is C raised and therefore called C sharp, whereas if it borrows from D, it is D lowered and is called D flat.

P 1 2   16.   An accidental affects all the notes on its own particular line or space for one complete measure, unless it is cancelled by another sign.

A SHARP	♯	raises a note by one semitone.
A FLAT	♭	lowers a note by one semitone.
A NATURAL	♮	cancels out a previous accidental, thus returning the note to its original pitch.
A DOUBLE SHARP	×	raises a note by two semitones, or a whole tone.
A DOUBLE FLAT	♭♭	lowers a note by two semitones, or a whole tone.

1 2

A group of one or more sharps or flats placed right after the clef sign is called a KEY SIGNATURE. This affects all the notes of those letter names throughout the piece, unless cancelled by another accidental. Key signatures are discussed further in Chapter 2, with regard to scales.

P 1 2   17.   When a semitone contains two notes with the same letter name, it is called a CHROMATIC SEMITONE.

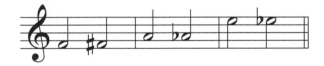

When a semitone contains two notes with different letter names, it is called a DIATONIC SEMITONE.

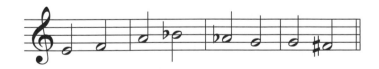

Remember: Diatonic and Different both start with a D!

16

P 1 2 EXERCISES

1. State whether each of the following is a diatonic semitone, a chromatic semitone, or a whole tone.

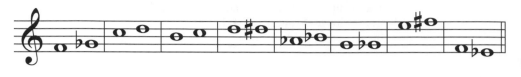

_____ _____ _____ _____ _____ _____ _____ _____

2. Write a chromatic semitone above each of the following notes.

3. Write a diatonic semitone above each of the following notes.

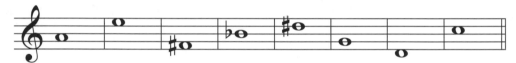

4. Write a chromatic semitone below each of the following notes.

5. Write a diatonic semitone below each of the following notes.

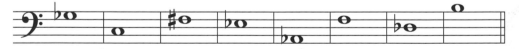

6. Give another name for each of the following notes.

a) F♯ _____   b) B♭ _____   c) C _____   d) A♭ _____   e) F _____   f) D♯ _____   g) D♭ _____

7. Name all the whole tones found between pairs of white keys on the piano.

_____

8. Name all the whole tones found between pairs of black keys on the piano.

_____

9.   Write a whole tone above each of the following notes.

10.   Write a whole tone below each of the following notes.

1 2   MORE EXERCISES

1.   Complete the following statements.

    a) To raise a ♮ one semitone, you use a _____.

    b) To lower a ♯ one semitone, you use a _____.

    c) To lower a ♮ two semitones, you use a _____.

    d) To raise a ♭ one semitone, you use a _____.

    e) To lower a ♮ one semitone, you use a _____.

    f) To raise a ♭ two semitones, you use a _____.

    g) To raise a ♯ one semitone, you use a _____.

    h) To lower a ♯ two semitones, you use a _____.

    i) To lower a ♭ one semitone, you use a _____.

    j) To raise a ♮ two semitones, you use a _____.

2.   Write a chromatic semitone above each of the following notes.

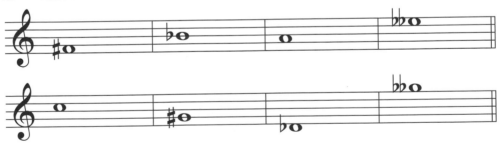

3.   Write a chromatic semitone below each of the following notes.

CHAPTER 2

MAJOR AND MINOR SCALES

MAJOR SCALES

P 1 2 1.   A SCALE is a series of notes arranged alphabetically and consecutively from any note to its octave. There are two kinds of scales in common use—DIATONIC and CHROMATIC.

A CHROMATIC scale ("chromatic" means colored) consists of all the twelve notes found between any note and its octave, all a semitone apart and all of equal importance. (This scale will be discussed later in Chapter 3.)

P 1 2 2.   A DIATONIC SCALE (diatonic means "according to the tonic") consists of only seven notes between any note and its octave, for example: C D E F G A B C. Notice that each of these seven notes has a different letter name. No letter is repeated, or skipped. Each has its own particular position in relation to the first note, which is the TONIC or keynote. These seven notes are spaced out in tones and semitones, and the order or arrangement of these tones and semitones can produce different kinds of diatonic scales:

      1. Major
      2. Minor
      3. Other Diatonic Modes (These will be discussed in Chapter 3.)

P 1 2 In all MAJOR SCALES, the tones (T) and semitones (ST) occur in the same order. The notes or DEGREES of a scale are numbered in arabic numerals capped with a carat sign (^).

Degrees of the scale:

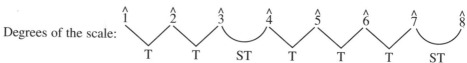

If we only use the white notes on the keyboard, it will be clearly seen that C is the only note we can start on to produce a major scale that has the tones and semitones in the correct order.

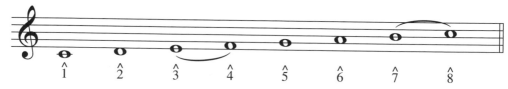

Notice, for example, that if we take G as the keynote, the second semitone is in the wrong place.

The F needs to be altered by raising it to F sharp, to make the necessary semitone between $\hat{7}$ and $\hat{8}$. It is very important that the letter names not be changed, so that they remain in alphabetical order, one note to each letter name.

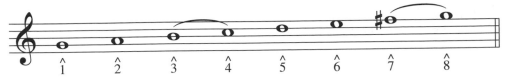

Similarly, if we use F as the keynote, the first semitone is in the wrong place,

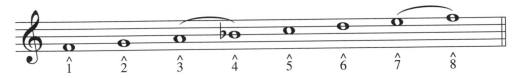

and a flat must be added to the B to make the required semitone between $\hat{3}$ and $\hat{4}$.

In both these scales, the semitones are now in the correct places to produce the sound of a major scale. From this we conclude that the key of G major contains one sharp: F sharp; and the key of F major contains one flat: B flat.

P 1 2   4.   For convenience, instead of writing an accidental in front of each F or each B as they occur throughout a piece, the sharps or flats are gathered together and placed at the beginning of each staff, right after the clef, showing that all the notes of their letter names are to be played as sharps or flats throughout, unless cancelled by another accidental. This group of accidentals is known as a KEY SIGNATURE.

For example, the scale of D major with a key signature instead of accidentals is written as follows:

P 1 2   5.   **MAJOR SCALES AND THEIR KEY SIGNATURES**

Memorize the following table.

No. of ♯'s or ♭'s	Sharp keys	Flat keys
0	C	
1	G	F
2	D	B♭
3	A	E♭
4	E	A♭
5	B	D♭
6	F♯	G♭
7	C♯	C♭

1 2

P 1 2   6.   There is an accepted order in which SHARPS must appear in key signatures:

F C G D A E B

The FLATS must appear in the reverse order:

B E A D G C F

Here is how they are placed on the staff:

2   In the alto and tenor clefs, they are placed as follows:

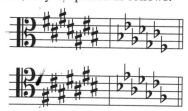

Opt.   7.   A scale may be divided into two halves, each of which is called a TETRACHORD. "Tetra" in Greek means four; tetrachord means four notes. A tetrachord, then, is half a scale—that is, the first four or the last four consecutive notes of each scale. In a major scale, the upper tetrachord has exactly the same order of tones and semitones as the lower one, and the two are separated by a whole tone.

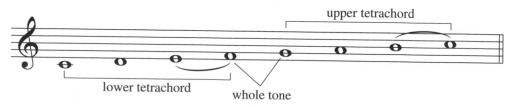

upper tetrachord

lower tetrachord   whole tone

P 1 2   NAMING DEGREES OF THE SCALE

8. The degrees of a scale may be numbered in arabic numerals capped with a carat sign or in Roman numerals.

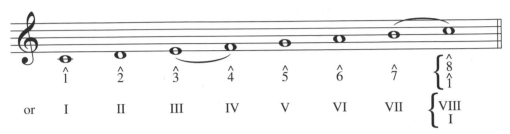

The most important note of any scale or key is, of course, the keynote or TONIC— the first degree of the scale.

Almost as important as the TONIC is the DOMINANT ($\hat{5}$ or V). This word is from the Latin "dominus," meaning master. As will be discussed later, the chord built on the dominant is so strong that it "masters" the key.

The fourth scale degree is called the SUBDOMINANT ($\hat{4}$ or IV). The Latin "sub" means under: the subdominant is the dominant five degrees BELOW the tonic, the "underdominant."

1 2   Here is a complete list of the TECHNICAL NAMES for the degrees of the scale.

$\hat{1}$ I   TONIC

$\hat{2}$ II   SUPERTONIC
The Latin "super" means above: the note above the tonic.

$\hat{3}$ III   MEDIANT
The Latin "medius" means middle: the middle note between the tonic and the dominant.

$\hat{4}$ IV   SUBDOMINANT

$\hat{5}$ V   DOMINANT

$\hat{6}$ VI   SUBMEDIANT
The third BELOW the tonic, midway between the tonic and the subdominant, the "undermediant."

$\hat{7}$ VII   LEADING NOTE
A note necessary to the identity of a key. The leading note is always a semitone below the tonic and leads directly to it.

P 1 2   EXERCISES

1. Write the following scales in the treble clef, ascending only, using accidentals instead of a key signature. Mark each semitone with a slur, and label the tonic, subdominant, and dominant notes.

a)   A major in half notes

b)   G major in dotted quarter notes

c)   F major in pairs of eighth notes

d)   E♭ major in whole notes

2. Write the following scales in the bass clef, ascending only, using the correct key signature for each. Mark each semitone with a slur, and label the tonic, subdominant, and dominant notes.

a)   D major in dotted half notes

b)   B♭ major in whole notes

c)   E major in quarter notes

d)   A♭ major in half notes

3. Write the following scales in the treble clef, ascending and descending, using accidentals instead of a key signature. Mark each semitone with a slur, and label the tonic, subdominant, and dominant notes.

a) E major in whole notes

b) Ab major in dotted half notes

c) C major in half notes

d) Bb major in pairs of eighth notes

e) D major in quarter notes

4. Write the following scales in the bass clef, ascending and descending, using the correct key signature for each. Mark each semitone with a slur, and label the tonic, subdominant, and dominant notes.

a) Eb major in half notes

b) G major in pairs of eighth notes

c) F major in dotted quarter notes

24

d)   A major in whole notes

5.   Write the following key signatures in the treble clef.
      a) Ab major   c) Bb major
      b) E major   d) D major

a)   b)   c)   d)

6.   Write the following key signatures in the bass clef.
      a) F major   c) Eb major
      b) A major   d) G major

a)   b)   c)   d)

7.   Write the following notes in the treble clef, using the correct key signature for each.
      a) the tonic of F major   e) the dominant of A major
      b) the tonic of Eb major   f) the dominant of G major
      c) the dominant of D major   g) the tonic of Ab major
      d) the subdominant of Bb major   h) the subdominant of E major

a)   b)   c)   d)   e)   f)   g)   h)

8.   Write the following notes in the bass clef, using the correct key signature for each.
      a) the tonic of E major   e) the dominant of Ab major
      b) the dominant of Bb major   f) the tonic of C major
      c) the subdominant of F major   g) the subdominant of G major
      d) the subdominant of D major   h) the dominant of Eb major

a)   b)   c)   d)   e)   f)   g)   h)

9. Write the following notes in the treble clef, using accidentals instead of key signatures.

a) the tonic of G major
b) the subdominant of F major
c) the dominant of D major
d) the dominant of B♭ major

e) the subdominant of C major
f) the tonic of B♭ major
g) the dominant of E major
h) the subdominant of E♭ major

a)   b)   c)   d)   e)   f)   g)   h)

10. Write the following notes in the bass clef, using accidentals instead of key signatures.

a) the tonic of A major
b) the dominant of C major
c) the dominant of E♭ major
d) the subdominant of G major

e) the subdominant of B♭ major
f) the dominant of F major
g) the subdominant of A major
h) the tonic of D major

a)   b)   c)   d)   e)   f)   g)   h)

11. Fill in the blanks in the following sentences.

a) The key signature of D major is _____.

b) The tonic of E♭ major is _____.

c) The key signature of A♭ major is _____.

d) The major key that has three sharps is _____.

e) _____ is the key signature of _____ major.

f) The major key that has two flats is _____.

g) The order of the first four sharps is _____.

h) Semitones occur between ___ and ___, and ___ and ___in every major scale.

i) The dominant of C major is _____.

j) The names of the flats in E♭ major are _____.

k) The key signature of E major is _____.

l) D is the subdominant of ___ major.

m) The major key that has four flats is _____.

n) The fifth note of any scale is called the _____.

o) A scale can be divided into two _____.

p) F is the dominant of _____ major.

q) 𝄢♭ is the key signature of _____ major.

r) The order of tones and semitones in every major scale is _____.

s) E♭ is the subdominant of _____ major.

t) The key that has no sharps or flats is _____ major.

1 2   MORE EXERCISES

1.   Write the following notes in the treble clef, using the correct key signature for each.

a) the mediant of B major

b) the dominant of F♯ major

c) the tonic of G♭ major

d) the submediant of D major

e) the supertonic of A major

f) the leading note of E♭ major

g) the subdominant of C♯ major

h) the dominant of A♭ major

i) the supertonic of B♭ major

j) the leading note of E major

a)   b)   c)   d)   e)

f)   g)   h)   i)   j)

2.   Write the following notes in the bass clef, using the correct key signature for each.

a) the tonic of D♭ major

b) the submediant of F major

c) the supertonic of C major

d) the dominant of E♭ major

e) the leading note of G major

f) the mediant of F♯ major

g) the subdominant of A major

h) the submediant of A♭ major

i) the mediant of B♭ major

j) the tonic of B major

a)   b)   c)   d)   e)

f)   g)   h)   i)   j)

3. Write the following notes in the treble clef, using accidentals instead of a key signature.

   a) the subdominant of C major
   b) the tonic of E♭ major
   c) the dominant of D major
   d) the mediant of A major
   e) the submediant of G major
   f) the dominant of B major
   g) the supertonic of A♭ major
   h) the leading note of C♯ major

a)   b)   c)   d)   e)   f)   g)   h)

4. Write the following notes in the bass clef, using accidentals instead of a key signature.

   a) the leading note of A major
   b) the supertonic of G♭ major
   c) the dominant of E major
   d) the submediant of B♭ major
   e) the median of C♯ major
   f) the leading note of B major
   g) the supertonic of D major
   h) the subdominant of G major

a)   b)   c)   d)   e)   f)   g)   h)

5. List the order of the sharps as they appear in a key signature.

6. List the order of the flats as they appear in a key signature.

7. Name the major key and the technical degree name of each of the following.

key:

degree:

key:

degree:

28

8. Name the major key and the technical degree name of each of the following.

key: _____ _____ _____ _____ _____ _____

degree: _____ _____ _____ _____ _____ _____

key: _____ _____ _____ _____

degree: _____ _____ _____ _____

9. Write the following scales, ascending and descending, in the treble clef.
   Use accidentals instead of a key signature, and mark the semitones with slurs.

a) F♯ major in half notes

b) C♭ major in quarter notes

c) D♭ major in eighth notes

10. Write the following scales, ascending and descending, in the treble clef. Use the
    correct key signature for each, and mark the semitones with slurs.

a) C♯ major in sixteenth notes

b) B major in half notes

c)   Gb major in whole notes

11.   Write the following scales, ascending and descending, in the bass clef. Use accidentals instead of a key signature, and mark the semitones with slurs.

a)   B major in quarter notes

b)   C♯ major in eighth notes

c)   Gb major in dotted half notes

12.   Write the following scales, ascending and descending, in the bass clef. Use the correct key signature for each, and mark the semitones with slurs.

a)   F♯ major in dotted quarter notes

b)   Db major in whole notes

c)   Cb major in sixteenth notes

13. Write the following scales in the treble clef, ascending only. Use the correct key signature for each. Use whole notes.

   a) the major scale whose key signature is five flats
   b) the major scale whose dominant is G♯
   c) the major scale whose leading note is A♯
   d) the major scale whose key signature is six flats
   e) the major scale whose supertonic is G♯
   f) the major scale whose mediant is E♭
   g) the major scale whose subdominant is F♯
   h) the major scale whose submediant is G♯
   i) the major scale whose leading note is F
   j) the major scale whose mediant is G

a)   b)

c)   d)

e)   f)

g)   h)

i)   j)

2   STILL MORE EXERCISES

1. Write the following scales in the alto clef, ascending and descending. Use the correct key signature for each, and mark the semitones with slurs. Use whole notes.

a)   B♭ major

b)   D major

c)   G♭ major

d)   C♯ major

e)   F major

f)   B major

g)   E♭ major

2.   Write the following scales in the alto clef, ascending and descending. Use accidentals instead of a key signature, and mark the semitones with slurs. Use whole notes.

a)   A major

b)   D♭ major

c)   F♯ major

d)   C major

e)   A♭ major

f)   E major

g)   G major

3.   Write the following scales in the tenor clef, descending only. Use the correct key signature for each, and mark the semitones with slurs. Use whole notes.

a) C major

b) E major

c) G major

d) A major

33

e) D♭ major

f) F♯ major

g) A♭ major

4. Write the following scales in the tenor clef, descending only. Use accidentals instead of a key signature, and mark the semitones with slurs. Use whole notes.

a) C♯ major

b) E♭ major

c) F major

d) B major

e) B♭ major

f) D major

g) G♭ major

5. Write the following scales in the bass clef, ascending and descending. Use the correct key signature, and mark the semitones with slurs. Use whole notes.

a) B♭ major, from dominant to dominant

b) E major, from supertonic to supertonic

c) D♭ major, from subdominant to subdominant

d) G major, from submediant to submediant

e) C♯ major, from tonic to tonic

6. Write the following scales in the treble clef, ascending and descending. Use accidentals instead of a key signature, and mark the semitones with slurs. Use whole notes.

a) A major, from mediant to mediant

b) F♯ major, from tonic to tonic

c) E♭ major, from dominant to dominant

d)   D major, from leading note to leading note

e)   B major, from supertonic to supertonic

7.   Write the following scales in the alto clef, ascending and descending. Use the correct key signature, and mark the semitones with slurs. Use whole notes.

a)   A♭ major, from dominant to dominant

b)   F♯ major, from leading note to leading note

c)   G♭ major, from supertonic to supertonic

d)   B major, from subdominant to subdominant

e)   A major, from submediant to submediant

8.   Write the following scales in the tenor clef, ascending and descending. Use accidentals instead of a key signature, and mark the semitones with slurs. Use whole notes.

a)   D♭ major, from tonic to tonic

b)   E major, from submediant to submediant

c)   F major, from mediant to mediant

d)   C♯ major, from supertonic to supertonic

e)   B♭ major, from leading note to leading note

MINOR SCALES

P 1 2   9.   At the beginning of this chapter, we noted two kinds of diatonic scales—major and minor. The word "minor" means smaller, and these scales are so called because in them the interval of a 3rd from $\hat{1}$ to $\hat{3}$ is one semitone smaller than the corresponding interval in major scales.

That is, there is a major 3rd between $\hat{1}$ and $\hat{3}$ of a major scale, but a minor 3rd between $\hat{1}$ and $\hat{3}$ of a minor scale. It is this difference in the third degree (the mediant) that immediately identifies a scale as being major or minor. (Intervals are discussed in Chapter 4.)

P 1 2   10.   Here is the lower tetrachord of C major, compared to that of C minor. Notice that the position of the semitone has shifted.

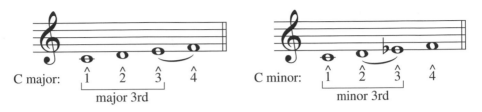

P 1 2   11.   Notice that, to begin with, we are making a comparison between a minor scale and its tonic major—that is, C minor as compared to C major. This is to enable you to hear and understand clearly the differences between the minor and major modes.

A major scale and a minor scale that share the same tonic, as here, are called TONIC MAJOR and TONIC MINOR. Thus, C major is the tonic major of C minor, and vice versa.

There are three kinds of minor scales, called NATURAL MINOR, HARMONIC MINOR, and MELODIC MINOR. The lower tetrachord is the same in all three kinds, but the upper tetrachord is different.

P 1 2   12.   **NATURAL MINOR**

In the natural minor scale, the sixth and seventh degrees, as well as the third degree, are one semitone lower than in its tonic major.

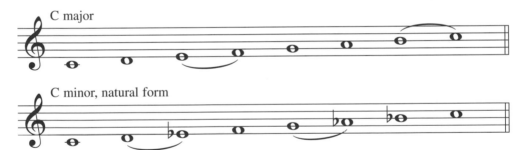

In the natural minor scale, semitones occur between $\hat{2}$ and $\hat{3}$ and between $\hat{5}$ and $\hat{6}$.

P 1 2   13.   Note that the natural minor scale has a whole tone between the seventh scale degree and the tonic. Only a note that is a semitone below the tonic is called a "leading note." When a whole tone separates these two notes, the seventh scale degree is called the SUBTONIC.

P 1 2   14.   HARMONIC MINOR

Of the three kinds of minor scales, this one is the most fundamental to a sense of the minor KEY. In the harmonic minor scale, the sixth degree as well as the third degree is one semitone lower than in its tonic major.

There are now three semitones in the harmonic minor: $\hat{2}$–$\hat{3}$, $\hat{5}$–$\hat{6}$, and $\hat{7}$–$\hat{8}$, and there is a distance of a tone-and-a-half or an augmented 2nd between $\hat{6}$ and $\hat{7}$. A careful study of this new order of tones and semitones, with particular attention to the position of the augmented 2nd, is of vital importance.

P 1 2   15.   MELODIC MINOR

As the name implies, the effect of this minor scale is more melodic in character. This is because in the upper tetrachord of the ascending scale, the slightly angular effect of the augmented 2nd is smoothed out by leaving the sixth degree as it is found in the tonic major, not lowering it as in the harmonic minor. In the descending scale, however, both $\hat{7}$ and $\hat{6}$ are lowered one semitone. Thus, there are two forms, one for ascending and one for descending. The lower tetrachord, as we have already said, is the same for both minors.

In the melodic minor scale, semitones occur between $\hat{2}$ and $\hat{3}$, and between $\hat{7}$ and $\hat{8}$ ascending, and between $\hat{6}$ and $\hat{5}$, and $\hat{3}$ and $\hat{2}$ descending.

Notice that the descending melodic minor scale sounds the same as the natural minor scale.

P 1 2   16.   MINOR KEY SIGNATURES

First it should be stated that the same key signature is used for all three forms of a minor scale—natural, harmonic, and melodic. An examination of the above examples in C minor will show that at different times both B natural and B flat are used for the seventh degree, and both A natural and A flat for the sixth degree. (E flat and the other degrees remain unchanged.) But the problem is that the method used for selecting an adequate key signature is at best a compromise—there can be no key signature that exactly meets all the requirements.

The solution to this dilemma is found by borrowing a key signature from the major that resembles it most closely. Thus, it will be clear that the E♭ major signature is the closest to C minor—in fact it can be used without any alteration for the natural form of C minor, and for the descending form of C melodic minor, being identical in every degree.

E♭ major

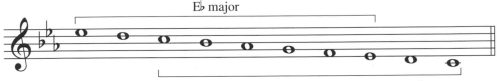

C minor, natural form and melodic descending

Thus, the key signature of E♭ major is placed at the beginning of a piece of music in C minor, and the accidentals affecting the sixth and seventh degrees are added where necessary.

C minor, natural form

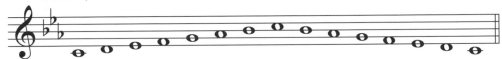

C minor harmonic

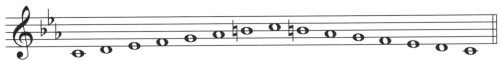

C minor melodic

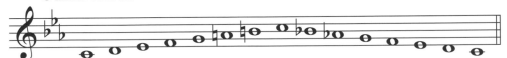

RELATIVE MAJORS AND MINORS

P 1 2   17.   A further study of these two scales—E♭ major and C minor—will show that:

* C is the sixth degree of E♭ major.
* E♭ is the third degree of C minor.
* The two tonic notes are a minor 3rd (or three semitones) apart.

E♭ major is called the RELATIVE MAJOR of C minor, and C minor is called the RELATIVE MINOR of E♭ major. That is, they both share the same key signature, and in that way are related.

Every minor has its relative major, and in order to write a minor scale it is first necessary to find what that relative major is, and thus to know the key signature.

The RELATIVE MAJOR of any minor key is found on the third note of that minor key. The RELATIVE MINOR of any major key is found on the sixth note of that major key. Therefore, to find the relative major, go up a 3rd, and to find the relative minor go down a 3rd, making sure in both cases that the new note is three semitones away from the old one.

Example 1. The relative minor of C major is found on $\hat{6}$ of C major (six notes up or better still three notes down), which is A. From A to C is three semitones, so A minor is the relative minor of C major, and has the same key signature of no sharps or flats.

Example 2. The relative major of A minor is found on $\hat{3}$ of A minor, which is C. Since from A to C is three semitones, C major is the relative major of A minor, and has the same key signature of no sharps or flats.

P 1 2   18.   **TABLE OF RELATIVE MAJOR AND MINOR KEYS**

Major	Sharp Keys	Minor
C		A
G		E
D		B
A		F♯
E		C♯
B		G♯
F♯		D♯
C♯		A♯

1 2

P 1 2

Major	Flat Keys	Minor

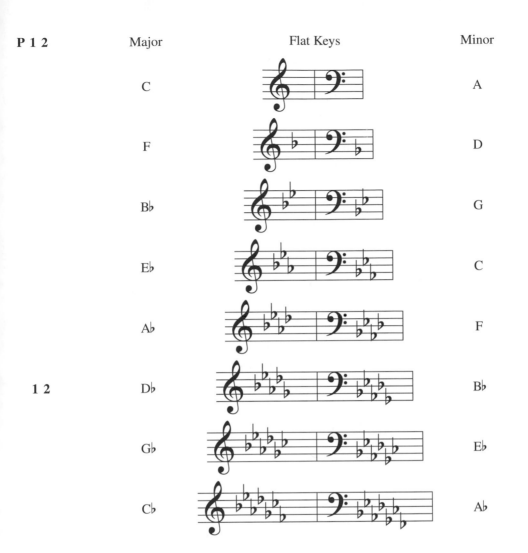

C	A
F	D
Bb	G
Eb	C
Ab	F
1 2 Db	Bb
Gb	Eb
Cb	Ab

P 1 2   19.   **NATURAL MINOR**

The natural minor scale sounds the same as its relative major scale starting from its sixth scale degree. When the natural minor scale is written using the key signature of its relative major, no additional accidentals are needed.

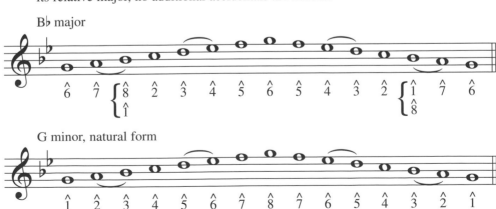

P 1 2   20.   To write either the harmonic or melodic form of the minor scale using the key signature of its relative major, certain adjustments need to be made by means of accidentals in order to produce the correct order of tones and semitones.

HARMONIC MINOR

Look again at the example of C minor harmonic on p. 39, and note again that the semitones are between $\hat{2}$–$\hat{3}$, $\hat{5}$–$\hat{6}$, and $\hat{7}$–$\hat{8}$, with the tone and a half between $\hat{6}$ and $\hat{7}$. A careful examination will show that only one note needs alteration—that is, $\hat{7}$, which has to be raised one semitone.

G minor harmonic (relative major: B♭)

MELODIC MINOR

Remembering the order of tones and semitones as seen in the example of C minor melodic on p. 39, we see that two notes need altering—$\hat{6}$ and $\hat{7}$—both of which must be raised one semitone in the ascending form, and lowered back again in the descending form.

G minor melodic (relative major: B♭)

SUMMARY

To write a natural minor scale, use the key signature of the relative major. No additional accidentals are needed.

To write a harmonic minor scale, use the key signature of the relative major, and raise the leading note one semitone without changing its letter name.

To write a melodic minor scale, use the key signature of the relative major, and raise $\hat{6}$ and $\hat{7}$ ascending, and lower them descending, without changing their letter names.

P 1 2   **EXERCISES**

1.   Name the relative major of the following minor keys.

     a)   C♯ minor _____   d)   B minor_____

     b)   A minor _____   e)   G minor_____

     c)   F minor _____   f)   E minor _____

2.   Name the relative minor of the following major keys.

     a)   A major _____   d)   E major _____

     b)   E♭ major _____   e)   G major_____

     c)   F major _____   f)   B♭ major _____

3.   Fill in the blanks in the following sentences.

     a)   The minor key whose key signature is one sharp is _____.

     b)   The key signature of B minor is _____.

     c)   The key signature of A major is _____.

     d)   The major key whose key signature is four flats is _____.

     e)   The subdominant of D minor is _____.

     f)   The minor key whose key signature is three sharps is _____.

     g)   The key signature of E♭ major is _____.

     h)   The dominant of F♯ minor is _____.

     i)   The major key whose key signature is two flats is _____.

     j)   The key signature of F minor is _____.

     k)   The minor key whose key signature is two flats is _____.

     l)   The major key whose key signature is one sharp is _____.

     m)   The key signature of C♯ minor is _____.

     n)   The dominant of B minor is _____.

     o)   The key signature of F major is _____.

     p)   The key signature of D minor is _____.

     q)   The major key whose key signature is four sharps is _____.

     r)   The minor key whose key signature is three flats is _____.

     s)   The key signature of D major is _____.

     t)   The subdominant of C♯ minor is _____.

4. Write the following scales in the treble clef, ascending and descending. Use the correct key signature for each, and mark the semitones with slurs. Use whole notes.

a) E minor, natural form

b) C minor, natural form

c) F♯ minor, natural form

5. Write the following scales in the treble clef, ascending and descending. Use the correct key signature for each, and label the tonic, subdominant, and dominant notes. Use whole notes.

a) A minor harmonic

b) C♯ minor harmonic

c) F minor harmonic

d) B minor harmonic

e) G minor harmonic

6. Write the following scales in the bass clef, ascending and descending.
    Use accidentals instead of a key signature. Use whole notes.

a) D minor melodic

b) E minor melodic

c) C minor melodic

d) F♯ minor melodic

7. Write the following scales in the treble clef, ascending and descending.
    Use accidentals instead of a key signature, and label the tonic, subdominant, and
    dominant notes. Use whole notes.

a) D minor, natural form

b) B minor, natural form

c) F minor, natural form

8.   Write the following scales in the bass clef, ascending and descending. Use the correct key signature and label the tonic, subdominant, and dominant notes. Use whole notes.

a)   C minor harmonic

b)   F♯ minor harmonic

c)   E minor harmonic

d)   D minor harmonic

9.   Write the following scales in the treble clef, ascending and descending. Use accidentals instead of a key signature. Use whole notes.

a)   B minor melodic

b)   G minor melodic

c)   A minor melodic

d)   C♯ minor melodic

10. Write the following scales in the bass clef, ascending and descending. Use the correct key signature for each, and mark the semitones with slurs. Use whole notes.

a) G minor, natural form

b) A minor, natural form

c) C♯ minor, natural form

d) F minor, natural form

11. Write the following scales in the treble clef, ascending and descending.
Use accidentals instead of a key signature, and mark the semitones with slurs.
Use whole notes.

a) E minor harmonic

b) D minor harmonic

c) F♯ minor harmonic

d) C minor harmonic

12. Write the following scales in the bass clef, ascending and descending. Use the correct key signature for each, and mark the semitones with slurs. Use whole notes.

a) B minor melodic

b) F minor melodic

c) C♯ minor melodic

d) G minor melodic

13. Write the following scales in the bass clef, ascending and descending. Use accidentals instead of a key signature, and mark the semitones with slurs. Use whole notes.

a) C♯ minor harmonic

b) F minor harmonic

c) A minor harmonic

d) G minor harmonic

14. Write the following scales in the treble clef, ascending and descending. Use the correct key signature for each, and mark the semitones with slurs. Use whole notes.

a) F♯ minor melodic

b) C minor melodic

c) D minor melodic

d) E minor melodic

1 2 MORE EXERCISES

1. Write the following scales in the treble clef, ascending and descending. Use the correct key signature for each, and mark the semitones with slurs. Use whole notes.

a) G♯ minor, natural form

b) the natural minor scale whose key signature is six flats

c) A♭ minor, natural form

d) the natural minor scale whose key signature is six sharps

2. Write the following scales in the bass clef, ascending and descending. Use accidentals instead of key signatures, and mark the semitones with slurs. Use whole notes.

a) B♭ minor, natural form

b) the natural minor scale whose relative major is E

c) A♯ minor, natural form

d) the natural minor scale whose relative major is A♭

3. Write the following scales in the treble clef, ascending and descending. Use the correct key signature for each, and mark the semitones with slurs. Use whole notes.

a) D♯ minor melodic

b) the melodic minor scale whose relative major is D♭

c) the melodic minor scale whose key signature is seven flats

4. Write the following scales in the treble clef, ascending and descending.
   Use accidentals instead of a key signature, and mark the semitones with slurs.
   Use whole notes.

a) A♯ minor melodic

b) the melodic minor scale whose relative major is G♭

c) the melodic minor scale whose key signature is five sharps

5. Write the following scales in the bass clef, ascending and descending, using
   accidentals instead of a key signature. Use whole notes.

a) B♭ minor melodic

b) the melodic minor scale whose relative major is F♯

c) the melodic minor scale whose key signature is seven flats

6. Write the following scales in the bass clef, ascending and descending, using the correct
   key signature for each. Use whole notes.

a) E♭ minor harmonic

b)   the harmonic minor scale whose relative major is B

c)   the harmonic minor scale whose key signature is seven sharps

7.   Write the following scales in the treble clef, ascending and descending, using the
       correct key signature for each. Use whole notes.

a)   A♭ major

       its relative minor, harmonic

       its tonic minor, melodic

b)   B♭ major

       its relative minor, melodic

       its tonic minor, harmonic

c)   F major

its relative minor, harmonic

its tonic minor, melodic

8.   Write the following scales ascending and descending, in the bass clef, using the correct key signature for each. Use whole notes.

a)   the melodic minor scale whose supertonic is D

b)   the harmonic minor scale whose dominant is B♭

c)   the melodic minor scale whose leading note is G♯

d)   the harmonic minor scale whose subdominant is E♭

e)   the harmonic minor scale whose mediant is A

9. Add the proper clef, key signature, and accidentals where necessary, to complete the following scales.

a) Gb major

b) E major

c) G minor melodic

d) Eb major

e) E minor harmonic

f) G# minor harmonic

2   STILL MORE EXERCISES

1. Write the following scales in the given clefs, ascending and descending. Use the correct key signature for each. Use whole notes.

a) Eb minor, natural form

b) C minor, natural form

c)   A♯ minor, natural form

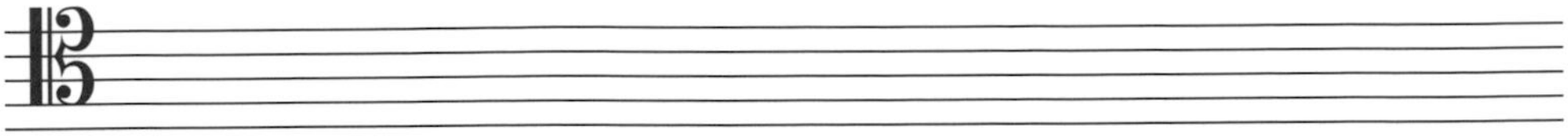

2.   Write the following scales in the given clefs, ascending and descending.
       Use accidentals instead of a key signature. Use whole notes.

a)   F minor, natural form

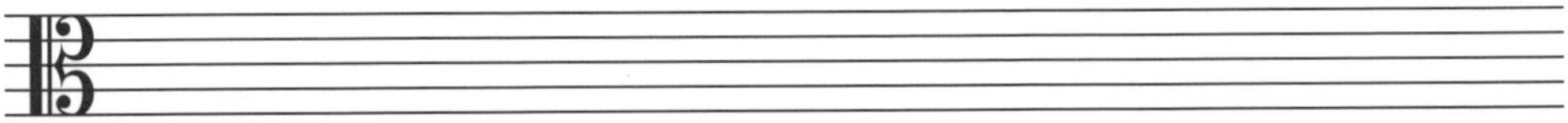

b)   G minor, natural form

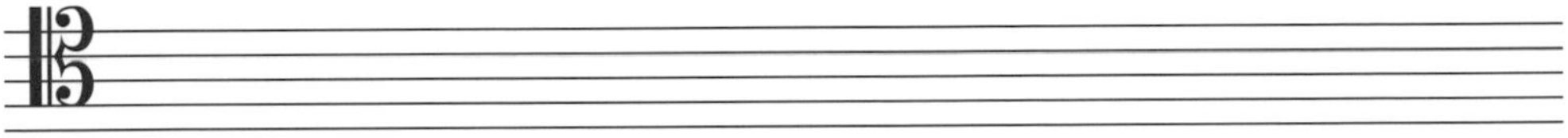

c)   C♯ minor, natural form

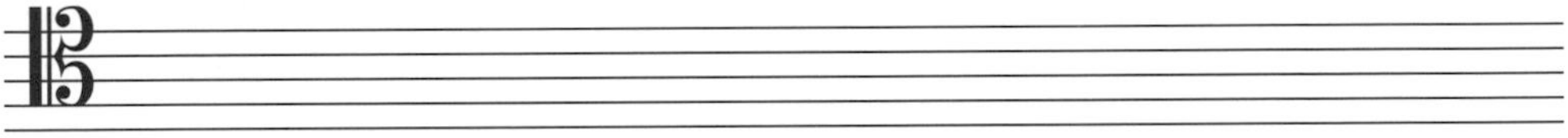

3.   Write the following scales in the alto clef, ascending and descending, using the
       correct key signature for each. Use whole notes.

a)   A♭ minor harmonic

b)   B minor melodic

c)   D♯ minor harmonic

d)   G minor harmonic

4.   Write the following scales in the tenor clef, ascending and descending, using the correct key signature for each. Use whole notes.

a)   C minor melodic

b)   G♯ minor harmonic

c)   E minor melodic

d)   F♯ minor melodic

5.   Write the following scales in the alto clef, ascending and descending, using accidentals instead of a key signature. Use whole notes.

a)   C minor harmonic

b)   E minor harmonic

c)   D minor melodic

d)   F♯ minor harmonic

6. Write the following scales in the tenor clef, ascending and descending, using accidentals instead of a key signature. Use whole notes.

a) B minor harmonic

b) E♭ minor harmonic

c) A♭ minor melodic

d) C♯ minor harmonic

7. Write the following scales in the given clefs, ascending and descending. Use the correct key signature for each. Use whole notes.

a) D♯ minor, natural form, from supertonic to supertonic

b) G♯ minor, natural form, from submediant to submediant

c) A♭ minor, natural form, from subdominant to subdominant

d) F♯ minor, natural form, from dominant to dominant

e) B♭ minor, natural form, from mediant to mediant

8. Write the following scales, ascending and descending, in the bass clef. Use the correct key signature for each, and mark the semitones with slurs. Use whole notes.

a) G♯ minor melodic, from dominant to dominant

b) C♯ minor harmonic, from subdominant to subdominant

c) E minor harmonic, from dominant to dominant

d) B♭ minor melodic, from tonic to tonic

e) F♯ minor harmonic, from subdominant to subdominant

9. Write the following scales in the alto clef, ascending and descending, using the correct key signature for each. Use whole notes.

a) A minor melodic, from subdominant to subdominant

b) F minor harmonic, from leading note to leading note

c) G♯ minor harmonic, from mediant to mediant

d)   B minor harmonic, from leading note to leading note

e)   C minor melodic, from supertonic to supertonic

f)   E♭ minor harmonic, from submediant to submediant

g)   D minor harmonic, from dominant to dominant

h)   F♯ minor melodic, from supertonic to supertonic

i)   B♭ minor harmonic, from subdominant to subdominant

10.   Write the following scales in the tenor clef, ascending and descending, using the correct key signature for each. Use whole notes.

a)   the major scale whose key signature is six sharps

b)   its relative minor, harmonic

c)   its tonic minor, melodic

11. Write the following scales in the bass clef, ascending and descending, using the correct key signature for each. Use whole notes.

a) the harmonic minor scale whose key signature is four sharps

b) its relative major

c) its tonic major

12. Add the proper clef, key signature, and accidentals where necessary to complete the following scales.

a) D major, from mediant to mediant

b) G minor melodic, from submediant to submediant

c) C♯ major, from submediant to submediant

d) F♯ minor harmonic, from tonic to tonic

e) A minor melodic, from tonic to tonic

f) E minor melodic, from mediant to mediant

g)   Bb major, from dominant to dominant

h)   C minor harmonic, from mediant to mediant

i)   F minor harmonic, from supertonic to supertonic

13.   Write the following scales in the treble clef, ascending and descending, using the correct key signature for each. Use whole notes.

a)   Eb major

b)   C minor, harmonic

c)   Eb minor, melodic

d)   D# minor, harmonic

State the relationship of the first scale in question 13 to each of the others.

relationship of a) to b) _____

relationship of a) to c) _____

relationship of a) to d) _____

CHAPTER 3

OTHER SCALES AND MODES

CHROMATIC SCALES

1 2 1. The term "scale" in its broadest sense means ladder, and thus means the orderly arrangement rising stepwise of all the main notes found in the music of a certain period of history or a certain country. The number of different scales that have been (and are being) used is enormous; therefore, you should in no way limit your thinking about scales to the basic diatonic major and minor scales used in Western art music.

As we mentioned in Chapter 2, a chromatic scale is one made up entirely of semitones. It has twelve different notes; the thirteenth note is an octave from the starting note. There are several different ways of notating the chromatic scale. Regardless of which method you use, the following two rules apply:

1. Begin and end on the same letter name. Do not change the starting note enharmonically (see p. 111).

2. No letter name may occur more than twice in a row. (For example, do not write D♭, D♮, D♯.)

1 2 2. **CHROMATIC SCALES USING ACCIDENTALS ONLY**

When a chromatic scale is written without using a key signature, accidentals are used to raise notes ascending and lower notes descending. A bar line at the top of the scale will cancel all the preceding accidentals and make it less complicated to write the descending scale.

If the starting note is a natural or sharp note, use sharps ascending and flats descending.

Example: chromatic scale on C

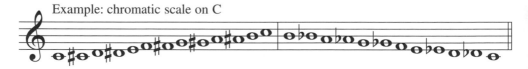

Example: chromatic scale on C♯

Notice that the final note is C♯ even though all the other accidentals in the descending scale are flats. This is because the starting note cannot be changed enharmonically.

If the starting note is a flat note, it may be necessary to use some flats or naturals going up because of the rule against using more than two of the same letter name in succession. Switch to sharps as soon as possible in the ascending scale.

Example: chromatic scale on D♭

1 2   3.   CHROMATIC SCALES USING KEY SIGNATURES

The chromatic scale can also be written with a key signature. Additional accidentals will be needed to form semitones; do not forget the sharps or flats in the key signature when writing the accidentals. A bar line after the top note of the scale will cancel all preceding accidentals but not the key signature.

A chromatic passage may occur in a piece of music that is in a major or minor key. The following examples show chromatic scales written with the key signature for the major scale with the same starting note.

To write a chromatic scale using the key signature of the tonic major scale, follow the steps outlined below.

1.   Write the key signature for the major key.

2.   Write the major scale, leaving spaces between each of the notes.

3.   Remember that the intervals between $\hat{3}$–$\hat{4}$ and $\hat{7}$–$\hat{8}$ of the major scale are already semitones.

4.   Fill in semitones between the other scale degrees: raise $\hat{1}$, $\hat{2}$, $\hat{4}$, $\hat{5}$, and $\hat{6}$ ascending, and lower $\hat{7}$, $\hat{6}$, $\hat{5}$, $\hat{3}$, and $\hat{2}$ descending.

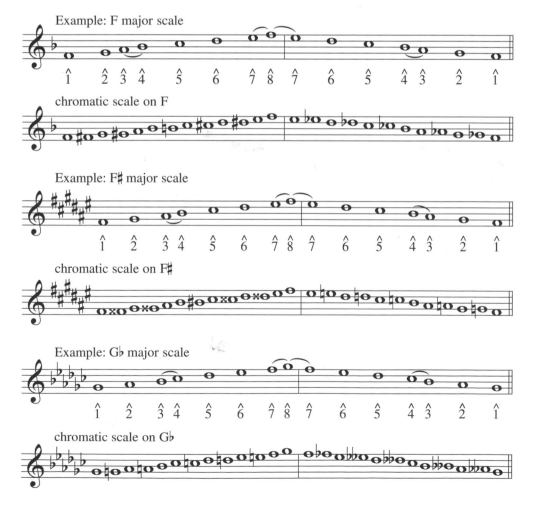

Example: F major scale

chromatic scale on F

Example: F♯ major scale

chromatic scale on F♯

Example: G♭ major scale

chromatic scale on G♭

1 2   EXERCISES

1. Write the following scales in the treble clef, ascending and descending, using accidentals. Use whole notes.

a)   chromatic scale starting on G

b)   chromatic scale starting on F

c)   chromatic scale starting on F♯

2. Write the following scales in the bass clef, ascending and descending, using accidentals. Use whole notes.

a)   chromatic scale starting on A

b)   chromatic scale starting on B

c)   chromatic scale starting on E♭

3. Add accidentals to each of the following to create chromatic scales.

a)

b)

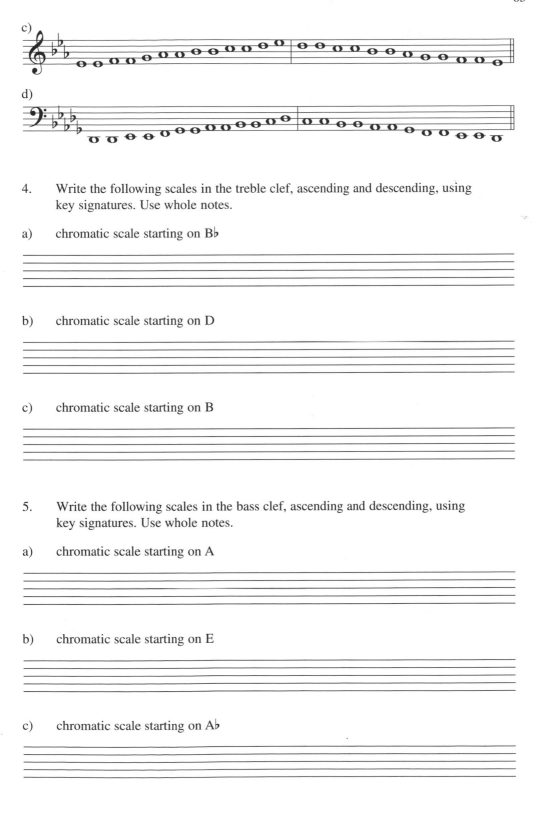

c)

d)

4.   Write the following scales in the treble clef, ascending and descending, using key signatures. Use whole notes.

a)   chromatic scale starting on B♭

b)   chromatic scale starting on D

c)   chromatic scale starting on B

5.   Write the following scales in the bass clef, ascending and descending, using key signatures. Use whole notes.

a)   chromatic scale starting on A

b)   chromatic scale starting on E

c)   chromatic scale starting on A♭

2 MORE EXERCISES

1. Write the following scales in the given clefs, ascending and descending, using accidentals. Use whole notes.

a) chromatic scale starting on F♯

b) chromatic scale starting on D

c) chromatic scale starting on B♭

d) chromatic scale starting on D♭

2. Write the following scales in the given clefs, ascending and descending, using key signatures. Use whole notes.

a) chromatic scale starting on C♯

b) chromatic scale starting on A♭

c) chromatic scale starting on E

d) chromatic scale starting on G♭

THE WHOLE TONE SCALE

1 2 4. Read the sections of Chapter 4 that deal with diminished intervals (p. 104) and with enharmonic equivalents (p. 111) before studying whole tone scales.

The WHOLE TONE SCALE is constructed entirely from notes a whole tone apart. It uses six different letter names. The seventh note, an octave from the starting note, must be spelled the same as the starting note. Do not change it enharmonically. In order for the scale to begin and end with the same letter name, it must contain one interval spelled as a diminished 3rd. The diminished 3rd (°3) is enharmonically equivalent to the major 2nd. The scale steps all *sound* the same size, even though one looks different.

The following scale has been written using only major 2nds. It sounds correct, but there are two problems with its notation:

• Seven different letter names have been used.
• The first and last notes are spelled differently.

incorrect:

To correct this, either the top or the bottom note must be respelled enharmonically. For example, we could change the top note of the scale above.

The major 2nd becomes a diminished 3rd.

Now the scale is notated correctly:

The diminished 3rd may occur at any one point in the scale. The example above could also be notated as follows.

Remember, to write a whole tone scale:

- Use six different letter names.
- Start and end on the same letter name.
- All steps will be major 2nds except for one step, which will be a diminished 3rd.

Since the notes of the whole tone scale are all the same distance apart, any one of them could be the tonic. It should be apparent that another whole tone scale could be constructed on C♯ (or D♭). This also could have six tonics. Because of this ambiguity of tonic, the scale has a curious vagueness of tonality. It was much used by Debussy, but after him its limitations seemed to be pretty well exhausted and it is seldom used today. ("Voiles" by Debussy is an example that uses both the whole tone scale and the pentatonic scale.)

1 2   EXERCISES

1. Change each of the following major 2nds into a diminished 3rd by respelling one of its notes enharmonically.

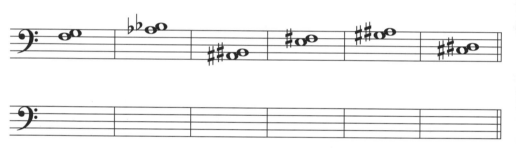

2. Change each of the following diminished 3rds into a major 2nd by respelling one of its notes enharmonically.

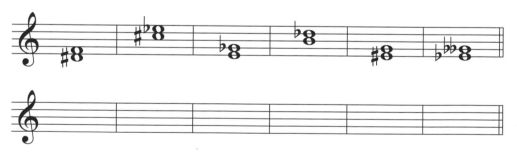

3. Add accidentals to each of the following to create whole tone scales. Do not alter the first note of each scale.

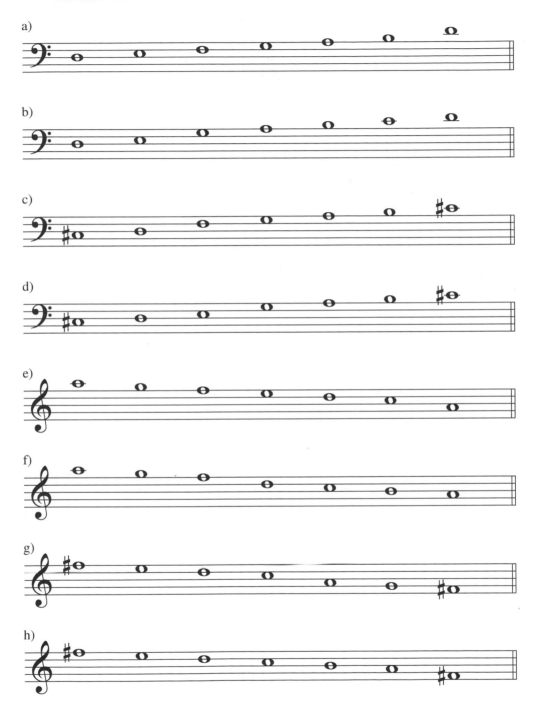

4. Write a whole tone scale in the treble clef, ascending and descending, beginning on each of the following notes.

a) on D

b) on E♭

c) on B

d) on G♭

5. Write a whole tone scale in the bass clef, ascending and descending, beginning on each of the following notes.

a) on A

b) on E

c) on F♯

d) on C♯

2 MORE EXERCISES

1. Write a whole tone scale in the tenor clef, ascending and descending, beginning on each of the following notes.

a) on D♭

b) on F♯

c) on A

d) on B♭

2. Write a whole tone scale in the alto clef, ascending and descending, beginning on each of the following notes.

a) on G

b) on A♭

c) on C♯

d) on B

THE BLUES SCALE

1 2 5. The blues originated as a style of African-American secular music.

Blues music was originally an oral tradition. Blues singers use pitches that cannot be notated precisely. These "blue notes" or "bent pitches" are slightly flattened notes on the third, fifth, and seventh scale degrees. In written music, the BLUES SCALE may be notated as follows:

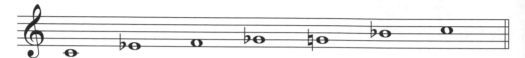

The easiest way to remember the structure of the blues scale is to memorize the interval formed between each note and the tonic.

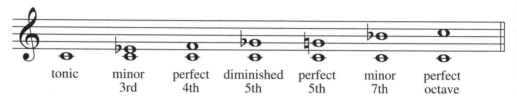

tonic	minor 3rd	perfect 4th	diminished 5th	perfect 5th	minor 7th	perfect octave

The diminished 5th may alternatively be spelled as an augmented 4th.

augmented 4th

1 2 **EXERCISES**

1. Add accidentals to each of the following to create blues scales. Do not alter the first note of each scale.

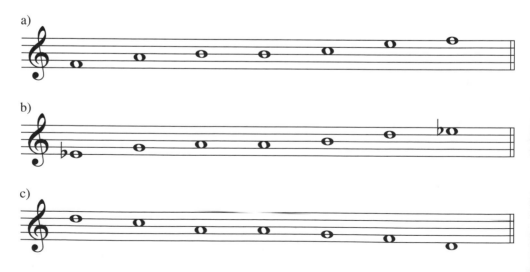

2. Write the following blues scales, in the treble clef, ascending only.

a) on G

b) on A♭

c) on C♯

3. Write the following blues scales in the bass clef, descending only.

a) on E

b) on F♯

c) on B♭

2 MORE EXERCISES

1. Write the following blues scales in the given clefs, ascending only.

a) on D♭

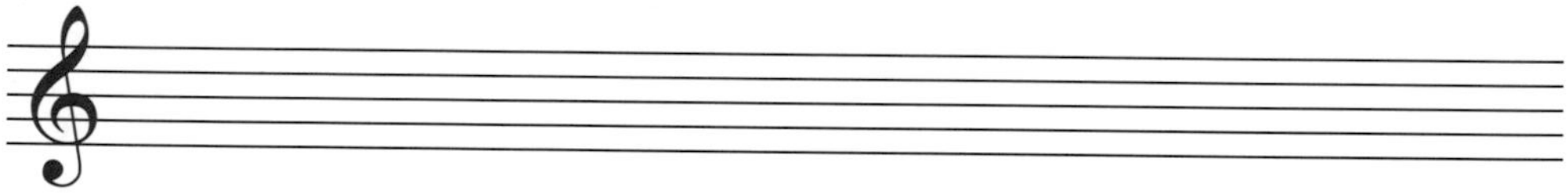

b) on E

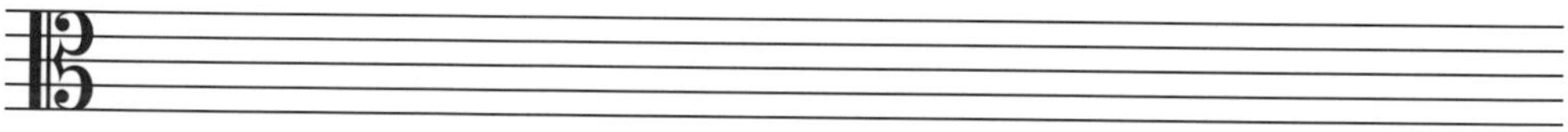

c) on E♭

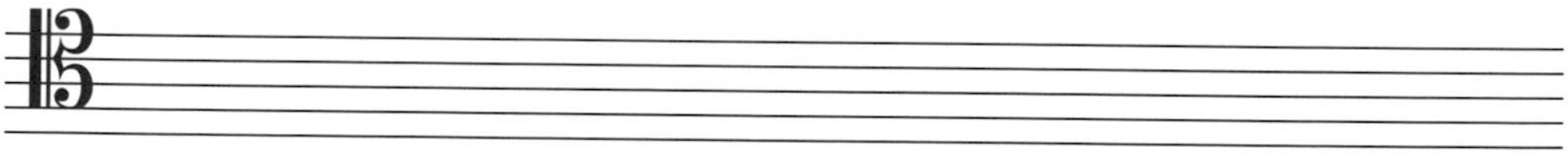

d) on F♯

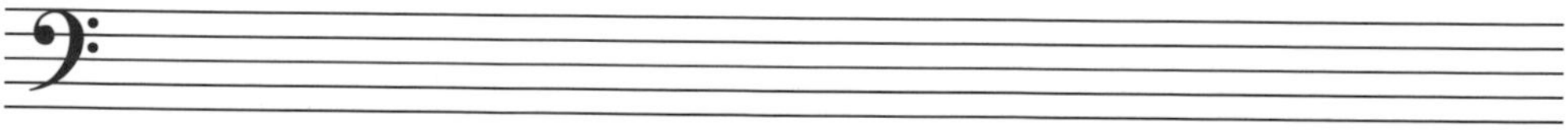

2.   Write the following blues scales in the given clefs, descending only.

a)   on A♭

b)   on B♭

c)   on C♯

d)   on B

THE OCTATONIC SCALE

1 2   6.   The OCTATONIC SCALE appears in the music of some 19th-century Russian composers, most notably Rimsky-Korsakov. This scale became more prevalent in the 20th century, occurring in works by composers such as Scriabin, Stravinsky, and Bartók; it is also used in jazz.

The octatonic scale has eight different notes ("octa" means eight). The ninth note, an octave from the starting note, must be spelled the same as the starting note; do not change it enharmonically. The octatonic scale is made of whole tones and semitones occurring in strict alternation. There are two different forms of the octatonic scale.

One form begins with a whole tone followed by a semitone; this pattern is then repeated until the octave is reached.

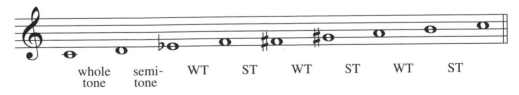

whole   semi-   WT   ST   WT   ST   WT   ST
tone   tone

The other form begins with a semitone followed by a whole tone, and so on.

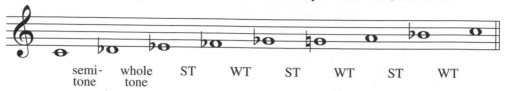

semi-   whole   ST   WT   ST   WT   ST   WT
tone   tone

The actual spelling of the octatonic scale is variable; the semitones may be spelled either as minor 2nds (diatonic semitones) or as augmented unisons (chromatic semitones).

This is the same scale as the second of the two examples above, but several notes have been changed enharmonically.

1 2   EXERCISES

1.   Add accidentals to each of the following to create octatonic scales. Do not alter the first *two* notes of each scale.

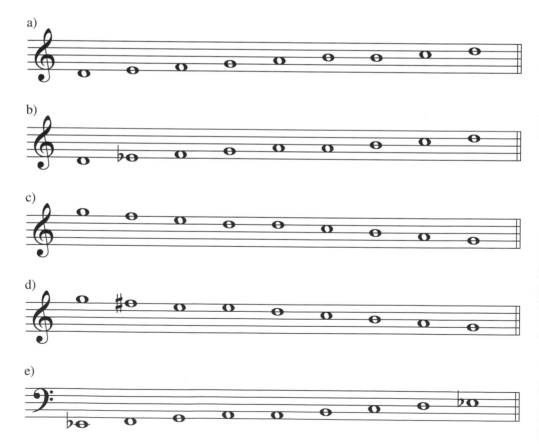

f)

g)

h)

2. Write each of the following octatonic scales in the bass clef, ascending and descending.

a) on E, starting with a semitone

b) on F, starting with a whole tone

c) on A♭, starting with a whole tone

d) on C♯, starting with a semitone

3. Write each of the following octatonic scales in the treble clef, ascending and descending.

a) on B, starting with a whole tone

b) on C, starting with a semitone

c) on F♯, starting with a whole tone

d) on B♭, starting with a semitone

2   MORE EXERCISES

1. Complete each of the following octatonic scales.

a)

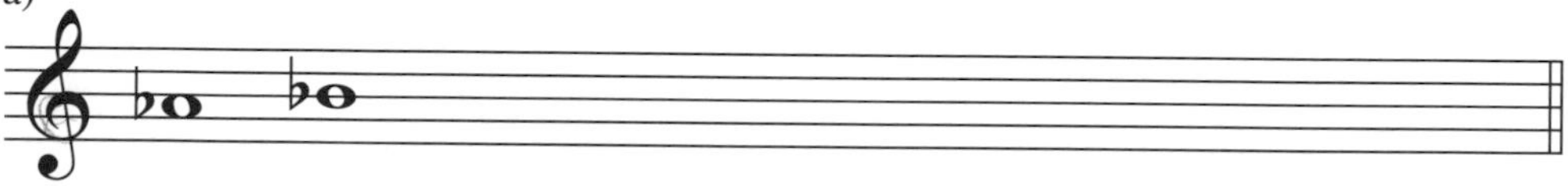

b)

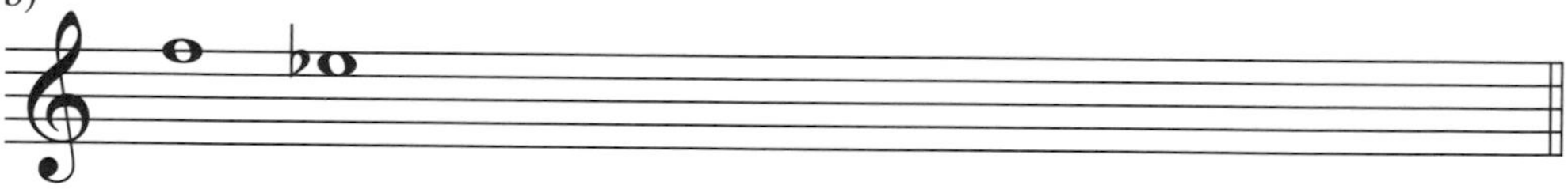

c)

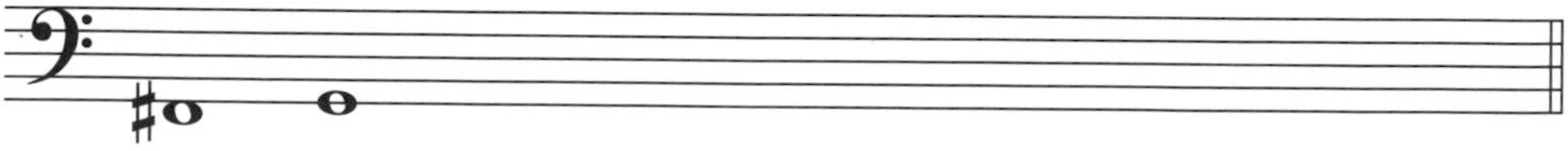

d)

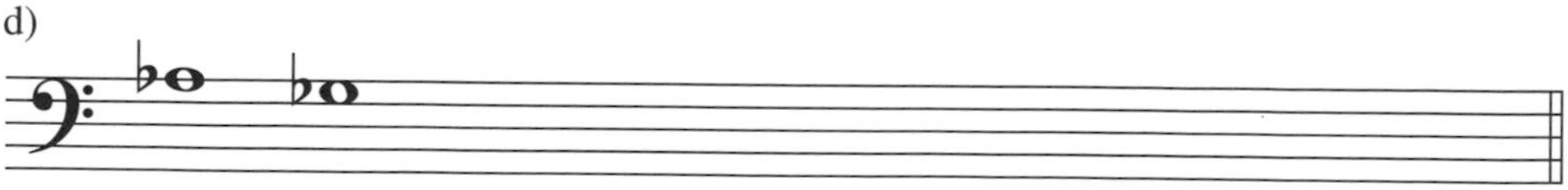

e)

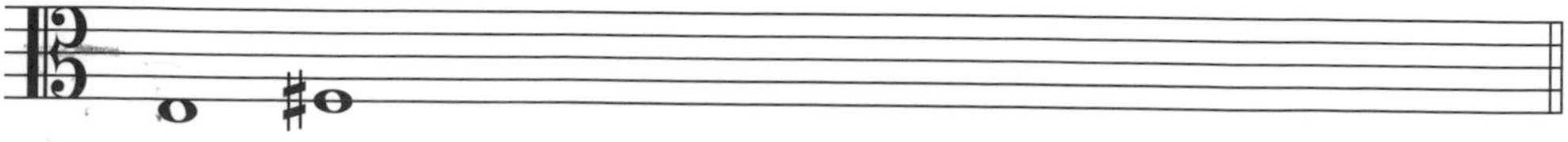

f)

g)

h)

Opt. The octatonic scale is also known as the DIMINISHED SCALE.

A diminished 7th chord (°7) is a chord consisting of a root, a minor 3rd, a diminished 5th, and a diminished 7th. (See Seventh Chords, p. 146.)

Example:

Any two diminished 7th chords that are *not* enharmonically equivalent will produce the notes of an octatonic scale.

The following octatonic scale consists of the notes found in the A°7 and B°7 chords:

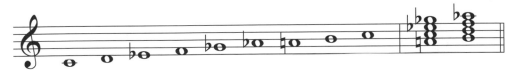

The following octatonic scale consists of the notes found in the B°7 and C♯°7 chords:

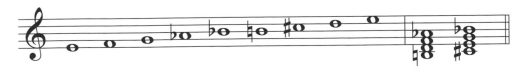

SUGGESTED EXERCISE: For each of the octatonic scales you have written in the preceding exercises, identify two diminished 7th chords that contain all the notes of the scale.

THE PENTATONIC SCALE

1 2 **7.** The PENTATONIC scale occurs in Asian music as early as 2000 BC and must be considered the prototype of all scales. It has been used as the basis of many folk tunes from around the world.

The pentatonic scale has five different notes ("penta" means five). The sixth note is the octave from the starting note. There are many different forms of pentatonic scales, using different intervals. Only the most common form is discussed here.

This form of the pentatonic scale uses only major 2nds and minor 3rds. Memorize the following pattern of intervals:

major   major   minor   major   minor
2nd   2nd   3rd   2nd   3rd

This form of the pentatonic scale may be played using only the black keys of the piano, starting on F♯ (or G♭).

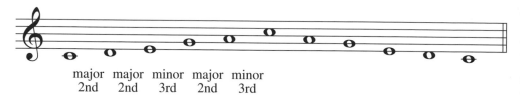

This scale may also be constructed by omitting the fourth and seventh degrees of a major scale. The key signature of the major scale may be used when writing the pentatonic scale.

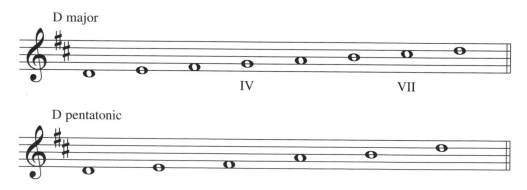

1 2   EXERCISES

1.   Write the following pentatonic scales in the treble clef, ascending and descending, using accidentals.

a)   on G

b)   on E♭

c)   on C♯

d)   on B♭

2.   Write the following pentatonic scales in the bass clef, ascending and descending, using accidentals.

a)   on F

b)   on A♭

c)   on G♭

d)   on E

3. Write the following major scales in the treble clef, ascending only, using the correct key signature for each. Then write pentatonic scales starting on the same notes and using the same key signatures.

Example: G major   G pentatonic

a) A major   G pentatonic

b) D♭ major   D♭ pentatonic

c) F♯ major   F♯ pentatonic

d) E major   E pentatonic

4. Write the following major scales in the bass clef, descending only, using the correct key signature for each. Then write pentatonic scales starting on the same notes and using the same key signatures.

a) D major   D pentatonic

b) B♭ major   B♭ pentatonic

c) E♭ major   E♭ pentatonic

2 MORE EXERCISES

1. Write the following pentatonic scales in the given clefs, ascending and descending, using accidentals.

a)   on B

b)   on A♭

c)   on E

d)   on D♭

2. Write the following pentatonic scales in the given clefs, ascending and descending, using the key signature of the tonic major scale for each.

a)   on G♭

b)   on E♭

c)   on F♯

d)   on A

MODES

2 8. Thousands of years ago, the ancient Greeks used scales built on tetrachords, and called them modes. These modes were used throughout Europe in the Medieval and Renaissance periods in both sacred and secular music. They fell out of favor during the Baroque, Classical, and Romantic eras, when they were largely replaced by the major and minor scales. Twentieth-century composers continued to use major and minor scales, but they also explored a large number of other scales. We have already studied the whole tone, chromatic, blues, octatonic, and pentatonic scales. In addition to these, 20th-century composers also began using the modes again.

2 9. These modes, like the major and minor scales covered in Chapter 2, are diatonic. Each mode uses seven different letter names. (The eighth note is an octave above the starting note.) The diatonic modes can be easily reproduced by using only the white keys on the piano, starting each mode on a different note. The note on which the mode begins and ends is called the "final."

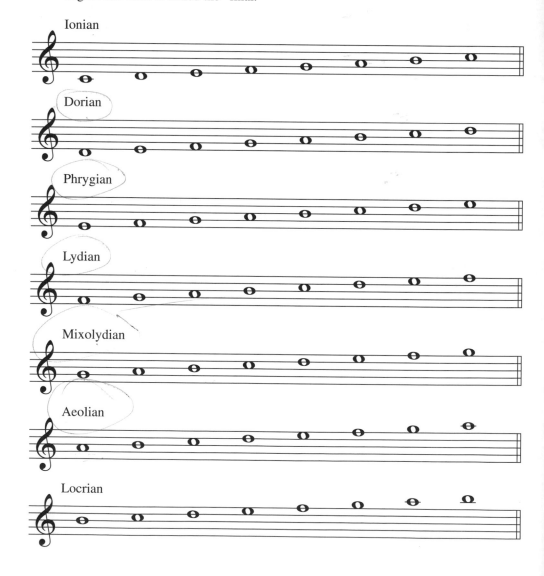

You can see from the above examples that the Ionian mode has the same pattern of tones and semitones as the major scale, and the Aeolian mode is like the natural minor scale. The Locrian mode is rarely used. Here, we will concentrate on the remaining four modes: Dorian, Phrygian, Lydian, and Mixolydian.

2 10. TONES AND SEMITONES IN THE MODES

Modes may be written using accidentals, using key signatures, or with a combination of both. Since notational practice in 20th-century music varies widely, you should memorize the pattern of tones and semitones in each mode. This will enable you to identify a mode in a piece of music, regardless of how the composer has notated it.

In the Dorian mode, semitones occur between $\hat{2}$ and $\hat{3}$, and between $\hat{6}$ and $\hat{7}$:

In the Phrygian mode, semitones occur between $\hat{1}$ and $\hat{2}$, and between $\hat{5}$ and $\hat{6}$:

In the Lydian mode, semitones occur between $\hat{4}$ and $\hat{5}$, and between $\hat{7}$ and $\hat{8}$:

In the Mixolydian mode, semitones occur between $\hat{3}$ and $\hat{4}$, and between $\hat{6}$ and $\hat{7}$:

2 **11.** **MODES COMPARED TO MAJOR SCALES STARTING ON VARIOUS DEGREES**

Dorian mode

The Dorian mode on D has the same structure as the C major scale written from supertonic to supertonic. A Dorian mode beginning on *any* note can be compared to some major scale starting on its supertonic note.

Example:

- To write the Dorian mode on C, find the major scale whose supertonic note is C.
- If C is $\hat{2}$, then $\hat{1}$ is B♭.
- Write the B♭ major scale from supertonic to supertonic. This can be done either using the accidentals B♭ and E♭ or using the key signature of B♭ major.

Phrygian mode

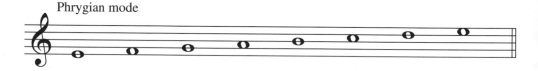

The Phrygian mode on E has the same structure as the C major scale written from mediant to mediant. A Phrygian mode beginning on any note can be compared to some major scale starting on its mediant note.

Example:

- To write the Phrygian mode on C, find the major scale whose mediant note is C.
- If C is $\hat{3}$, then $\hat{1}$ is A♭.
- Write the A♭ major scale from mediant to mediant, using either accidentals or the A♭ major key signature.

Lydian mode

The Lydian mode on F has the same structure as the C major scale written from subdominant to subdominant. A Lydian mode beginning on any note can be compared to some major scale starting on its subdominant note.

Example:

- To write the Lydian mode on C, find the major scale whose subdominant note is C.
- If C is $\hat{4}$, then $\hat{1}$ is G.
- Write the G major scale from subdominant to subdominant, using either accidentals or the G major key signature.

Mixolydian mode

The Mixolydian mode on G has the same structure as the C major scale written from dominant to dominant. A Mixolydian mode beginning on any note can be compared to some major scale starting on its dominant note.

Example:

- To write the Mixolydian mode on C, find the major scale whose dominant note is C.
- If C is $\hat{5}$, then $\hat{1}$ is F.
- Write the F major scale from dominant to dominant, using either accidentals or the F major key signature.

2 10. MAJOR AND MINOR MODES

Another way of looking at modes is to class them as major or minor based on the interval from their tonic to their mediant.

The Dorian and Phrygian modes have minor 3rds:

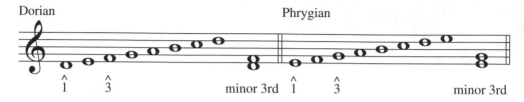

The Lydian and Mixolydian modes have major 3rds:

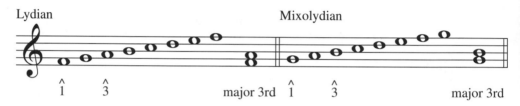

Dorian mode

The Dorian mode on D is similar to the D minor scale, natural form, but with a raised submediant scale degree. Key signatures that are based on comparing the Dorian mode to its tonic minor scale follow these principles:

- Sharp keys use the key signature of the tonic minor, and $\hat{6}$ is raised with an accidental.

- Flat keys use the key signature of the tonic minor, but with one less flat than usual. (The *last* flat in the minor key signature is omitted.)

Phrygian mode

The Phrygian mode on E is similar to the E minor scale, natural form, but with a lowered supertonic scale degree. Key signatures that are based on comparing the Phrygian mode to its tonic minor scale follow these principles:

- Sharp keys use the key signature of the tonic minor, but with the last sharp omitted.

- Flat keys use the key signature of the tonic minor, and $\hat{2}$ is lowered with an accidental.

Phrygian mode on F♯   Phrygian mode on F

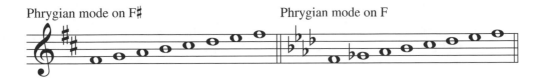

Lydian mode

The Lydian mode on F is similar to the F major scale, but with a raised subdominant scale degree. Key signatures that are based on comparing the Lydian mode to its tonic major scale follow these principles:

- Sharp keys use the key signature of the tonic major, and $\hat{4}$ is raised with an accidental.

- Flat keys use the key signature of the tonic major, but with the last flat omitted.

Lydian mode on E   Lydian mode on E♭

Mixolydian mode

The Mixolydian mode on G is similar to the G major scale, but with a lowered seventh scale degree. Key signatures that are based on comparing the Mixolydian mode to its tonic major scale follow these principles:

- Sharp keys use the key signature of the tonic major, but with the last sharp omitted.

- Flat keys use the key signature of the tonic major, and the seventh scale degree is lowered with an accidental.

2 EXERCISES

1. Write the following major scales in the given clefs, ascending and descending. Use the correct key signature and start on the specified degree for each scale. Identify the equivalent mode in each case.

Example: A major on $\hat{4}$ or ___Lydian mode on D___

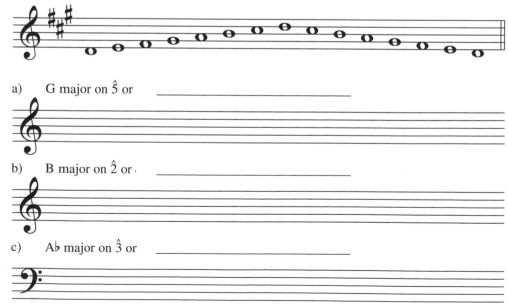

a)   G major on $\hat{5}$ or   _____

b)   B major on $\hat{2}$ or   _____

c)   A♭ major on $\hat{3}$ or   _____

d)   Bb major on $\hat{2}$ or   _____

e)   D major on $\hat{4}$ or   _____

f)   Eb major on $\hat{2}$ or   _____

g)   F major on $\hat{4}$ or   _____

h)   E major on $\hat{3}$ or   _____

2.   Write the following modes in the given clefs, ascending and descending.
      Use accidentals instead of key signatures. Identify the equivalent major scale and its
      starting degree in each case.

Example: Mixolydian mode on Bb or   _Eb major on $\hat{5}$_

a)   Phrygian mode on G or   _____

b)   Mixolydian mode on E or   _____

c)   Dorian mode on C or   _____

d)   Lydian mode on F♯ or   _____

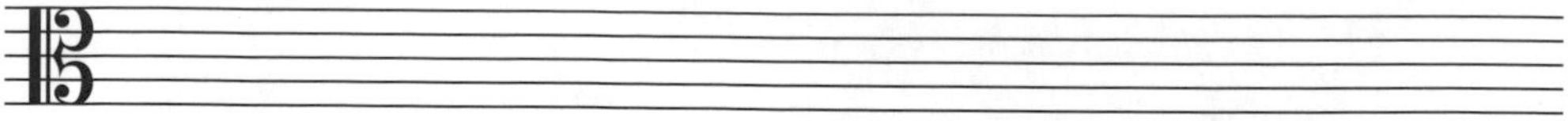

e)   Dorian mode on F♯ or   _____

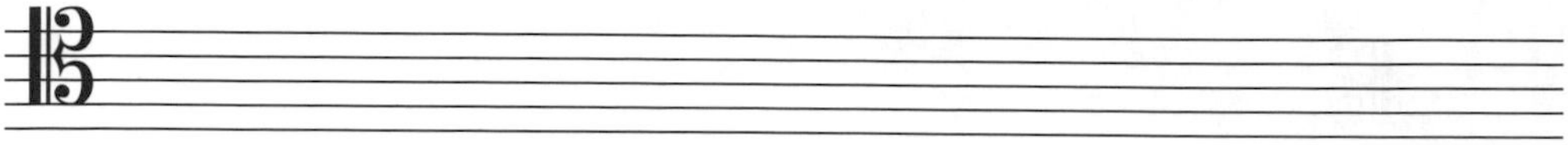

f)   Phrygian mode on C or   _____

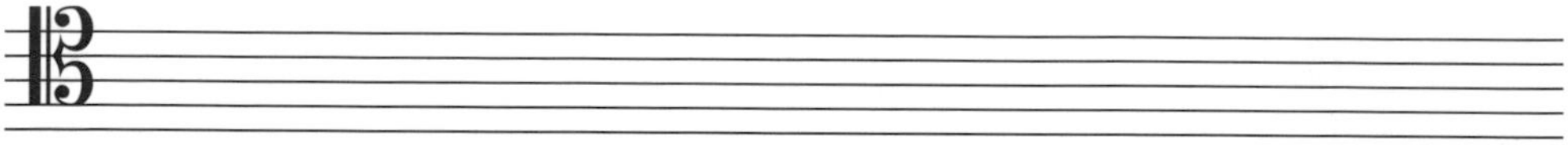

g)   Mixolydian mode on A or   _____

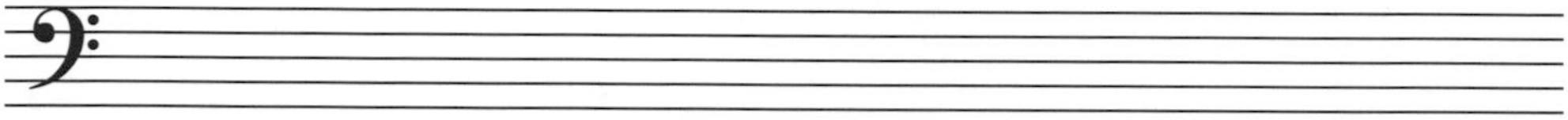

h)   Lydian mode on G♭ or   _____

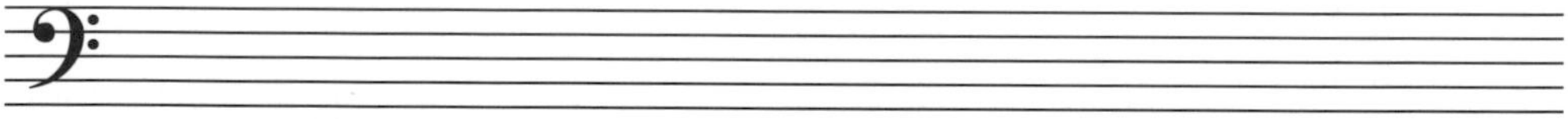

3.   Write the following modes in the given clefs, ascending and descending.
      Use key signatures and add any necessary accidentals, based on the principles
      outlined on pp. 88–90.

a)   Lydian mode on B♭

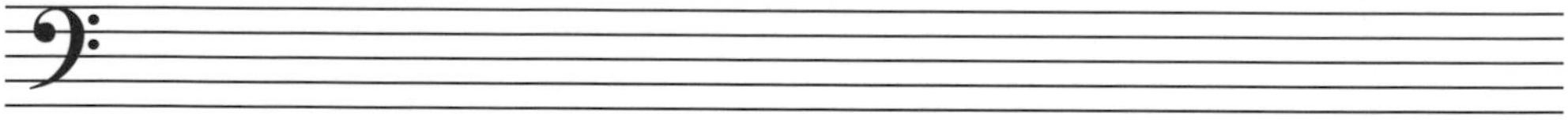

b)   Dorian mode on C

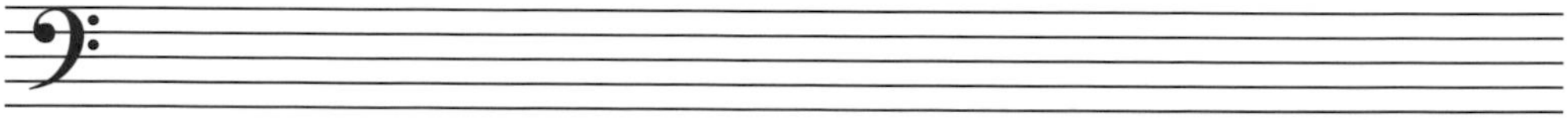

c)   Mixolydian mode on A♭

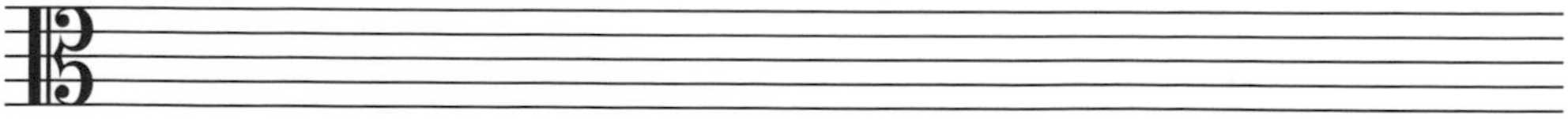

d)   Phrygian mode on F♯

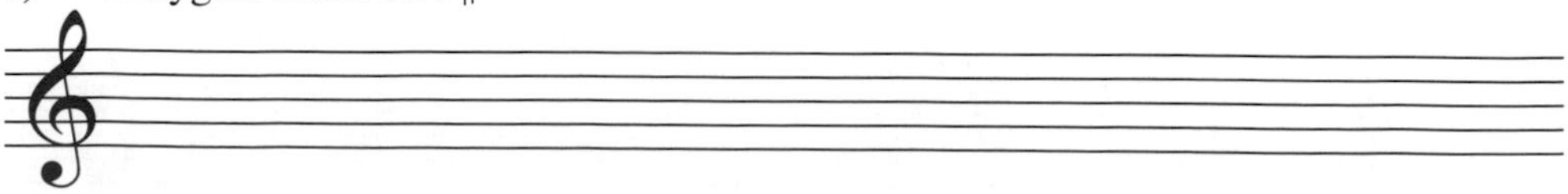

e)　Lydian mode on E

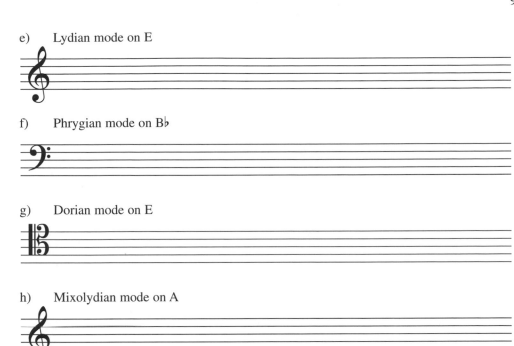

f)　Phrygian mode on B♭

g)　Dorian mode on E

h)　Mixolydian mode on A

1 2　REVIEW: IDENTIFYING SCALE TYPES

EXERCISES

1.　Name each of the following scales as major, natural minor, harmonic minor, melodic minor, whole tone, chromatic, blues, octatonic, or pentatonic.

a)

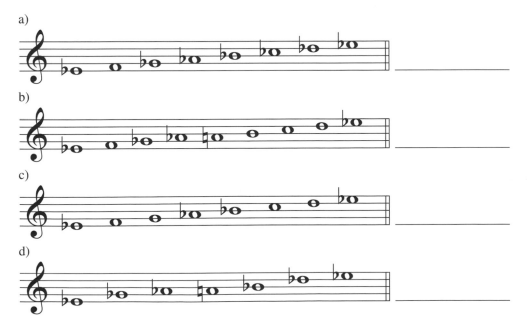

b)

c)

d)

e)

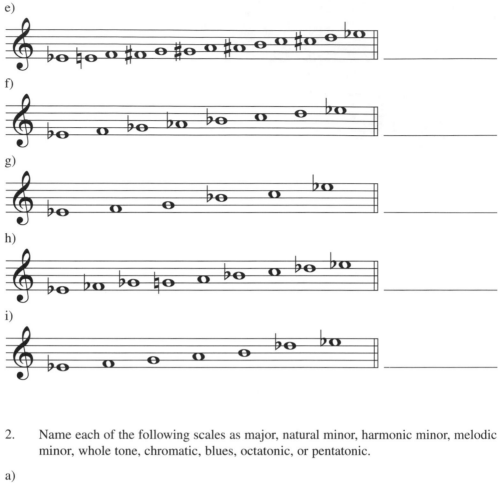

f)

g)

h)

i)

2. Name each of the following scales as major, natural minor, harmonic minor, melodic minor, whole tone, chromatic, blues, octatonic, or pentatonic.

a)

b)

c)

d)

e)

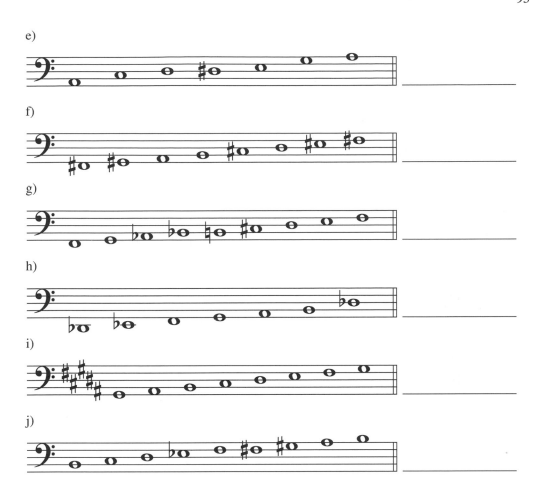

f)

g)

h)

i)

j)

3. Name each of the following scales as major, natural minor, harmonic minor, melodic minor, whole tone, chromatic, blues, octatonic, or pentatonic.

a)

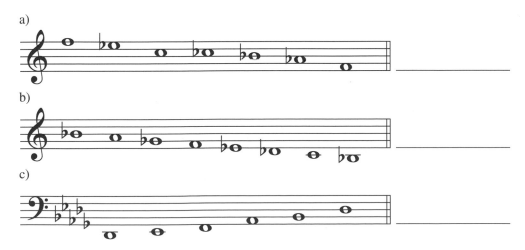

b)

c)

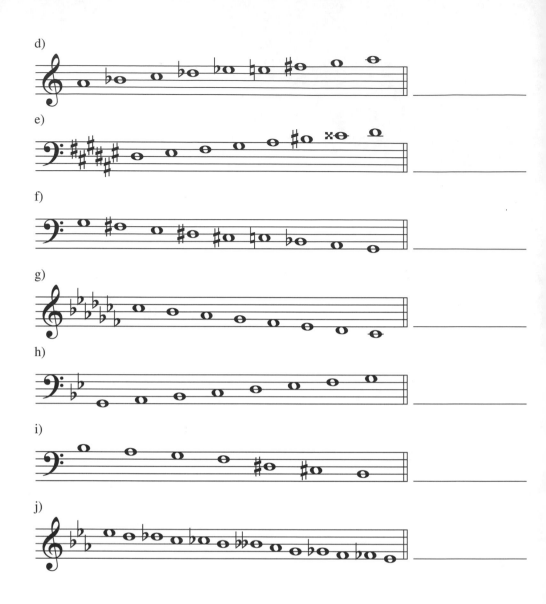

d)

e)

f)

g)

h)

i)

j)

2 MORE EXERCISES

1. Identify each of the following as major, minor (specify natural, harmonic, or melodic), whole tone, chromatic, blues, octatonic, or pentatonic scales, or as Dorian, Phrygian, Lydian, or Mixolydian modes. Assume that each example starts on its tonic.

a)

b)

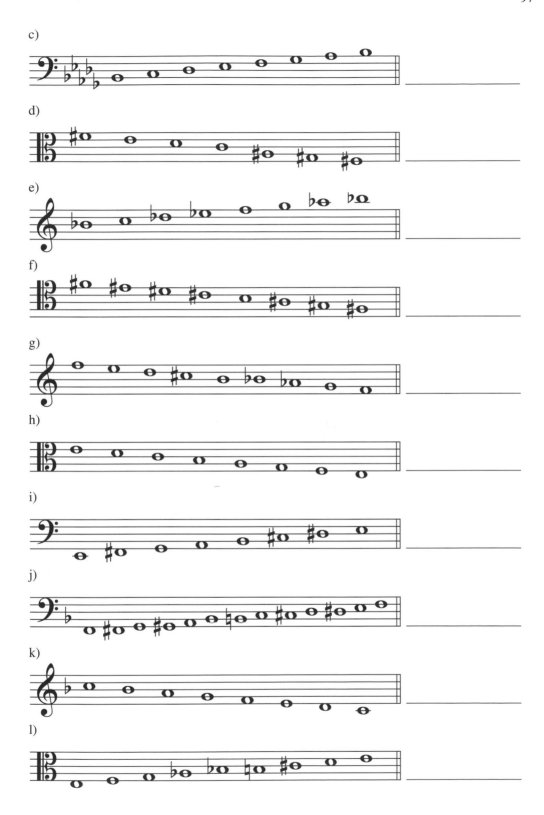

CHAPTER 4

INTERVALS

INTERVAL TYPE, SIZE, AND QUALITY

P 1 2   1.   An INTERVAL is the distance in pitch between two notes.

If the notes are played at the same time, the interval is HARMONIC.

If the notes are played one after, the other the interval is MELODIC.

In either case, the method of naming the interval is the same.

P 1 2   2.   The SIZE of an interval is measured by the number of letter names contained in the interval, including both the bottom and the top notes.

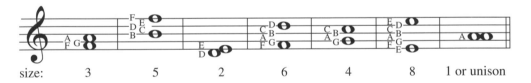

| size: | 3 | 5 | 2 | 6 | 4 | 8 | 1 or unison |

3.   These intervals are all 7ths:

It is obvious that as well as finding the size of the interval, you must also find exactly what the QUALITY of the interval is, that is, major, minor, and so on.

Consider the intervals found in a major scale. Using the scale of C major as an example, and building one of each interval in turn above the tonic note C, the intervals are numbered and described as follows:

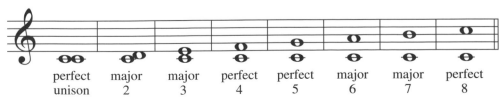

| perfect unison | major 2 | major 3 | perfect 4 | perfect 5 | major 6 | major 7 | perfect 8 |

Notice that the unison, 4th, 5th, and octave are called PERFECT, while the 2nd, 3rd, 6th, and 7th are called MAJOR. All intervals are named as if the lower note is, for that moment, the tonic. Thus, the intervals found in the A major scale (or any other major scale) will be precisely the same as those found in the C major scale.

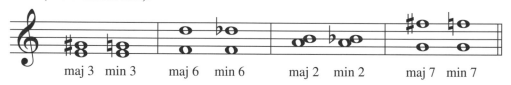

perfect	major	major	perfect	perfect	major	major	perfect
unison	2	3	4	5	6	7	8

This interval contains four letter names—F G A B—therefore, it is a 4th. Since the scale of F major has B♭ as its fourth note, the interval is a perfect 4th (commonly abbreviated as per 4).

This interval contains three letter names—G A B—therefore, it is a 3rd. Since the scale of G major has B as its third note, the interval is a major 3rd (maj 3).

This interval contains seven letter names—E F G A B C D—therefore, it is a 7th. Since the scale of E♭ major has a D as its seventh note, the interval is a major 7th (maj 7).

P 1 2   4.   If a major interval is made one semitone smaller, it becomes a MINOR interval (abbreviation: min).

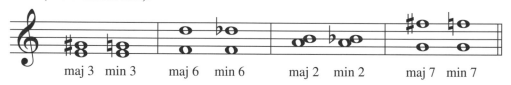

maj 3   min 3   maj 6   min 6   maj 2   min 2   maj 7   min 7

This interval contains six letter names—therefore, it is a 6th. Since the sixth note of the scale of E major is C sharp, this interval is one semitone smaller than a major 6th, i.e., a minor 6th.

This interval is a 3rd. Since the third note of the scale of F major is A, this is one semitone smaller than a major 3rd, i.e., a minor 3rd. (You have already encountered major and minor 3rds in studying minor scales.)

P 1 2   5.   Here are some intervals written in both their harmonic and melodic forms.

Harmonic intervals:

Melodic intervals:

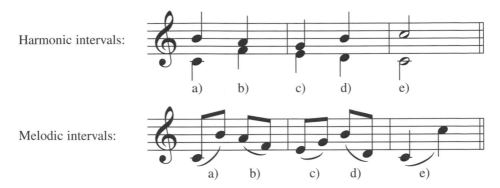

a)   The lower note is C. In the scale of C major, B is its seventh note. Therefore, it is a major 7th.

b)   The lower note is F. In the scale of F major, A is its third note. Therefore, it is a major 3rd.

c)   The lower note is E. In the scale of E major, G sharp is the third note. Therefore, it is one semitone smaller than a major 3rd, and is a minor 3rd.

d)   The lower note is D. In the scale of D major, B is its sixth note. Therefore, it is a major 6th.

e)   The lower note is C. In the scale of C major, C is its octave. Therefore, it is a perfect octave.

P 1 2   **EXERCISES**

1.   Name the following intervals. Use abbreviations: maj for major, min for minor, and per for perfect.

2.   Write the following intervals above the given notes.

a)   per 8   min 3   per 4   maj 7   min 6   maj 2   min 7   min 2

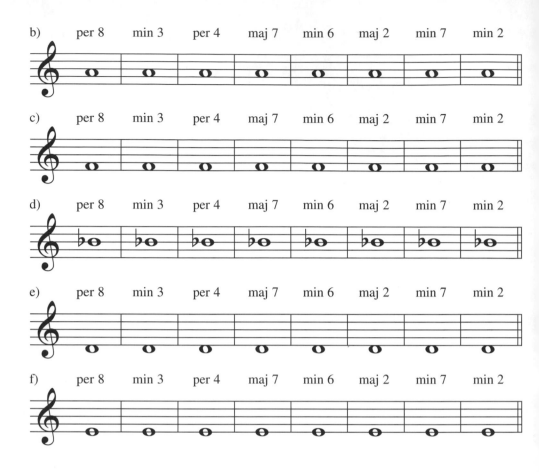

b) per 8   min 3   per 4   maj 7   min 6   maj 2   min 7   min 2

c) per 8   min 3   per 4   maj 7   min 6   maj 2   min 7   min 2

d) per 8   min 3   per 4   maj 7   min 6   maj 2   min 7   min 2

e) per 8   min 3   per 4   maj 7   min 6   maj 2   min 7   min 2

f) per 8   min 3   per 4   maj 7   min 6   maj 2   min 7   min 2

3.   Name the following intervals.

4.   Name the following intervals.

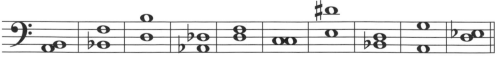

5. Write the following intervals above the given notes.

a)   maj 3   per 5   min 3   maj 6   min 2   per 4   min 6   per 1

b)   maj 3   per 5   min 3   maj 6   min 2   per 4   min 6   per 1

c)   maj 3   per 5   min 3   maj 6   min 2   per 4   min 6   per 1

d)   maj 3   per 5   min 3   maj 6   min 2   per 4   min 6   per 1

e)   maj 3   per 5   min 3   maj 6   min 2   per 4   min 6   per 1

f)   maj 3   per 5   min 3   maj 6   min 2   per 4   min 6   per 1

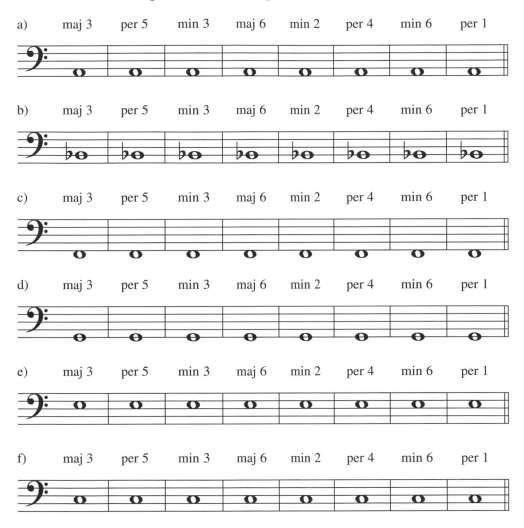

6. Name the following intervals.

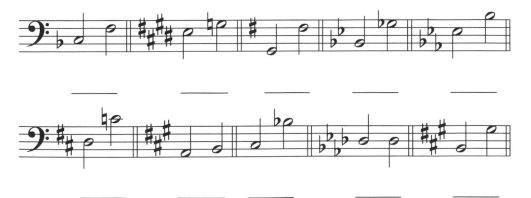

1 2 6.   A DIMINISHED interval is one semitone smaller than a perfect interval.

A DIMINISHED interval is also one semitone smaller than a minor interval, which makes it two semitones smaller than a major interval.

The abbreviation for diminished is dim: dim 3, dim 4, dim 5, etc.

1 2 7.   An AUGMENTED interval is one semitone larger than either a perfect or a major interval. (You have already encountered augmented 2nds in studying minor scales.)

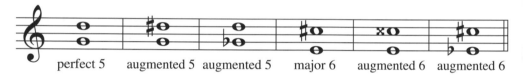

The abbreviation for augmented is aug: aug 5, aug 6, etc.

1 2 8.   **A SPECIAL CASE: THE UNISON**

A perfect unison is the smallest possible interval. Two notes of the same pitch have no distance between them. This interval cannot be made smaller, and therefore a unison is never diminished.

If we alter one of the notes in a perfect unison by lowering it a semitone, then the two notes in the interval become further away from each other and the interval is larger. The interval is now an augmented unison.

Remember: regardless of which note is written first, count from the lower pitched note to measure an interval. These are all augmented unisons:

1 2

Thus, there are two types of unisons: perfect (as they exist in the scale) and augmented (one semitone larger). There are three types of 4ths, 5ths, and octaves: perfect (as they exist in the scale), diminished (one semitone smaller), and augmented (one semitone larger); and four types of 2nds, 3rds, 6ths, and 7ths: major (as they exist in the major scale), minor (one semitone smaller), diminished (two semitones smaller), and augmented (one semitone larger).

To sum up: To solve any interval, first find its size (count its letters). Then see if the upper note exists in the major scale of the lower note. If it does, then the interval is either perfect or major depending on its size. If it does not, then compare how much smaller or larger it is than normal, and decide whether it is minor, diminished, or augmented.

1 2   10.   **UNUSUAL INTERVALS**

Occasionally you will find an interval whose bottom note cannot be considered as the tonic of a logical key, such as this one:

Example 1

For the moment, forget about the accidental on the bottom note and think of the interval as being in the key of E. E to G♯ is a major 3rd. Then replace the sharp on the E, thus making the notes closer together, and the interval one semitone smaller. The answer is a minor 3rd.

Example 2

Start by omitting the flat from the lower note and think of the interval in the scale of F major. F to D is a major 6th. Then replace the flat on the F, thus making the notes farther apart and making the interval one semitone larger. The answer is an augmented 6th.

When you replace the given accidental on the bottom note, pay careful attention to whether this makes the interval larger or smaller. If you raise the bottom note, this brings it closer to the top note, making the interval smaller. If you lower the bottom note, this takes it farther away from the top note, making the interval larger.

Opt.   11.   **CONSONANCE and DISSONANCE**

It is interesting to notice how much musical styles have changed over the years regarding intervals that are "consonant" and "dissonant." Traditionally, consonant refers to sounds that are satisfactory, or agreeable, in themselves. Consonant intervals are treated as stable and not requiring resolution. Dissonant means disagreeable, incomplete, demanding to be followed by a more satisfying sound called a resolution. Bear in mind that the quality of dissonance is its sense of movement, not its degree of unpleasantness.

Conventionally, the intervals considered to be consonant are all the perfect intervals, major and minor 3rds, and major and minor 6ths. All augmented and diminished intervals, and all 2nds and 7ths are considered dissonant. No really satisfactory definition has ever been found, however, because the whole concept of consonance and dissonance is always changing.

Historically, the 4th was the first interval accepted as consonant, with the 5th added as a consonance around the ninth or tenth century. The 3rd was admitted in the 14th century, and this radically changed the whole picture of harmony. Tertian harmony, harmony built on the triad, became the basis of "common practice" European music. However, with the ever-increasing use of dissonance by composers since around 1900, and the steady decline in the importance of the triad to the structure of harmony, any attempt to generalize about "pleasant" and "unpleasant" sounding intervals seems irrelevant.

INVERTED INTERVALS

1 2   12.   When an interval is turned upside down it is said to be INVERTED. The lower note then becomes the upper, and the upper note becomes the lower.

You can see from a study of the above examples that the size of the interval plus the size of its inversion equals 9. Also notice that when inverted:

- major intervals become minor
- minor intervals become major
- augmented intervals become diminished
- diminished intervals become augmented
- perfect intervals remain perfect

Use these simple rules as a means of checking the accuracy of your work, rather than as a short cut to naming intervals without really working them out.

1 2   13.   **A SPECIAL CASE: INVERTING THE AUGMENTED OCTAVE**

Since the augmented octave is bigger than the perfect octave, simply moving one of the notes up or down one octave will not invert the interval. (See Section 16 on pp. 111–112 on compound intervals.)

In the following examples, A♮ is always the lower note and A♯ is always the upper note; none of intervals is an inversion of the others.

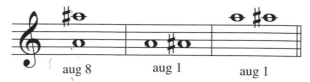

The following examples show inversions of the augmented octave. The interval is inverted when A♯ is the lower note. The octave in which the inversion is written is irrelevant.

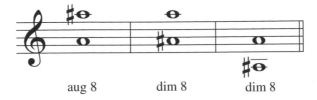

aug 8   dim 8   dim 8

Note that the method of checking your inversion by adding the numeric sizes does not work in the case of the augmented octave.

1 2   EXERCISES

1.   Write the following intervals above the given notes.

108

2. Write the following intervals above the given notes.

a) maj 6 aug 2 dim 3 min 7 aug 5 dim 4 min 2 per 8

b) maj 6 aug 2 dim 3 min 7 aug 5 dim 4 min 2 per 8

c) maj 6 aug 2 dim 3 min 7 aug 5 dim 4 min 2 per 8

d) maj 6 aug 2 dim 3 min 7 aug 5 dim 4 min 2 per 8

e) maj 6 aug 2 dim 3 min 7 aug 5 dim 4 min 2 per 8

f) maj 6 aug 2 dim 3 min 7 aug 5 dim 4 min 2 per 8

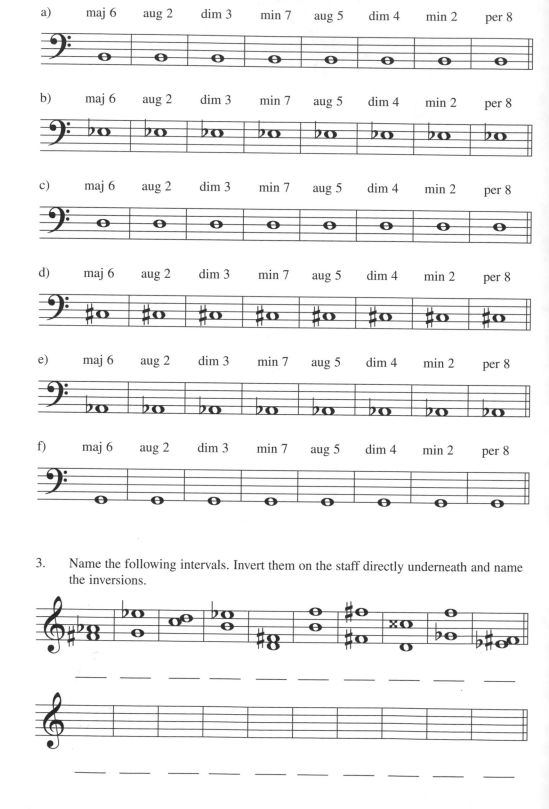

3. Name the following intervals. Invert them on the staff directly underneath and name the inversions.

4.   Name the following intervals. Invert them and name the inversions.

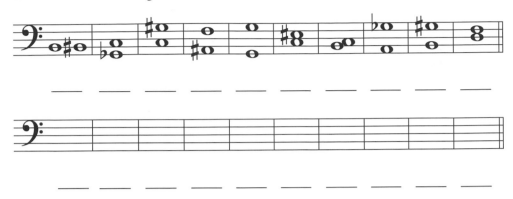

_____ _____ _____ _____ _____ _____ _____ _____ _____ _____

5.   Write the following intervals above the given notes. Invert them and name the inversions.

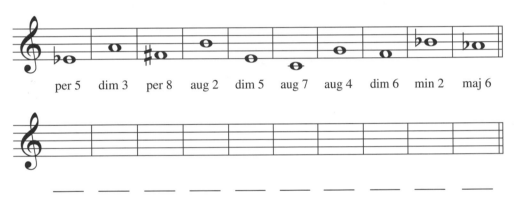

per 5   dim 3   per 8   aug 2   dim 5   aug 7   aug 4   dim 6   min 2   maj 6

_____ _____ _____ _____ _____ _____ _____ _____ _____ _____

6.   Write the following intervals above the given notes. Invert them and name the inversions.

dim 7   per 5   min 7   aug 6   min 3

_____ _____ _____ _____ _____

7. Name the following intervals. Invert them in the bass clef and name the inversions.

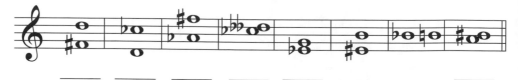

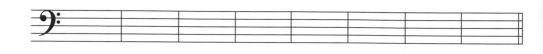

MORE ABOUT INTERVALS

2 14. WRITING AN INTERVAL BELOW A GIVEN NOTE

So far, all of the exercises in which you were asked to write a specific interval gave the bottom note and asked you to write the top note. If you are asked to write a specific interval below a given note, use the following steps to find the bottom note.

Example 1. Write a major 7th below E.

1. Find the correct letter name for the lower note. Check the required *size* of the interval and count down from the given note. A 7th below E is F.

2. Check the *quality* of the interval resulting from Step 1. F to E is a major 7th, so in this case, no further steps are necessary.

Example 2. Write an augmented 4th below D.

1. Find the correct letter name for the lower note. A 4th below D is A.

2. Check the *quality* of the interval you have written. A to D is a perfect 4th. An augmented 4th is required, so it is necessary to make the interval one semitone bigger by adding an accidental to the bottom note.

3. Lower A♮ to A♭, to create an augmented 4th below D.

Example 3. Write a diminished 3rd below C♯.

1. A 3rd below C♯ is A.

2. A to C♯ is a major 3rd. A diminished 3rd is required, so you need to make the interval two semitones smaller.

3. Raise A♮ to A♯, to create a diminished 3rd below C♯.

2 15. ENHARMONIC CHANGE

When you change a note enharmonically, you change its name, without changing its pitch:

These two intervals 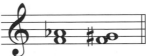 sound exactly the same, and appear the same on the piano, and yet the name of the first is a minor 3rd, while the second is an augmented 2nd. Similarly, when you change the upper note of this interval enharmonically, you have an interval that is, for our purposes here, identical in pitch, but which has an entirely different name:

dim 5   aug 4

2 16. COMPOUND INTERVALS

A COMPOUND INTERVAL is any interval that is larger than an octave. The best way to solve one is to bring the top note down one or more octaves, thereby reducing the interval to its simple form, within an octave. The compound interval will be the same as the simple interval plus 7.

Example. This interval is an 11th.

When reduced to its simple form, it becomes a perfect 4th.

The correct name of the compound interval is a perfect 11th. It is also called a compound perfect 4th. Be careful when you invert this. Remember that the G must end up as the lower note of the inversion. The resulting inversion is a perfect 5th. The octave in which your answer is written does not matter.

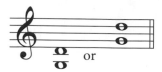

2   17.   FINDING THE SCALES CONTAINING A GIVEN INTERVAL

In order to find the scales containing a given interval, you must first find where the interval exists within the required scale types. In the following exercises, we will consider three scale types: major, natural minor, and harmonic minor.

Suppose the interval in question is a major 3rd.

First, build 3rds on every degree of a major scale, a natural minor scale, and a harmonic minor scale. In this example, C major and minor scales are used, although any scales would be suitable.

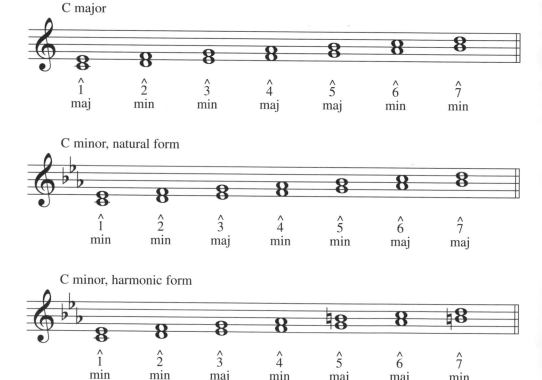

You will find that major 3rds occur on $\hat{1}$, $\hat{4}$, and $\hat{5}$ of major scales, on $\hat{3}$, $\hat{6}$, and $\hat{7}$ of natural minor scales, and on $\hat{3}$, $\hat{5}$, and $\hat{6}$ of harmonic minor scales.

Therefore, the lower note of any given major 3rd will be the $\hat{1}$, $\hat{4}$, and $\hat{5}$ degrees of the major scales that contain it, the $\hat{3}$, $\hat{6}$, and $\hat{7}$ degrees of the natural minor scales that contain it, and the $\hat{3}$, $\hat{5}$, and $\hat{6}$ degrees of the harmonic minor scales that contain it.

If the given interval is

then F is: $\hat{1}$ of F major, $\hat{4}$ of C major, and $\hat{5}$ of B♭ major

     $\hat{3}$ of D minor (nat), $\hat{6}$ of A minor (nat), and $\hat{7}$ of G minor (nat)

     $\hat{3}$ of D minor (har), $\hat{5}$ of B♭ minor (har), and $\hat{6}$ of A minor (har)

Similar tables may be constructed for any interval.

To summarize, the steps are:

- Solve the interval.
- Construct tables using one major scale, one natural minor scale, and one harmonic minor scale to discover on which degrees of the scales similar intervals occur.
- Using these degrees, count down from the lower note of the given interval to find the tonic of the keys in which the interval occurs.

2 EXERCISES

1. Name the following intervals.

2. Name the following intervals.

114

3. Write the following intervals above the given notes.

a) min 2 dim 7 aug 3 maj 6 dim 4 per 5 aug 2 min 7 per 1 maj 3

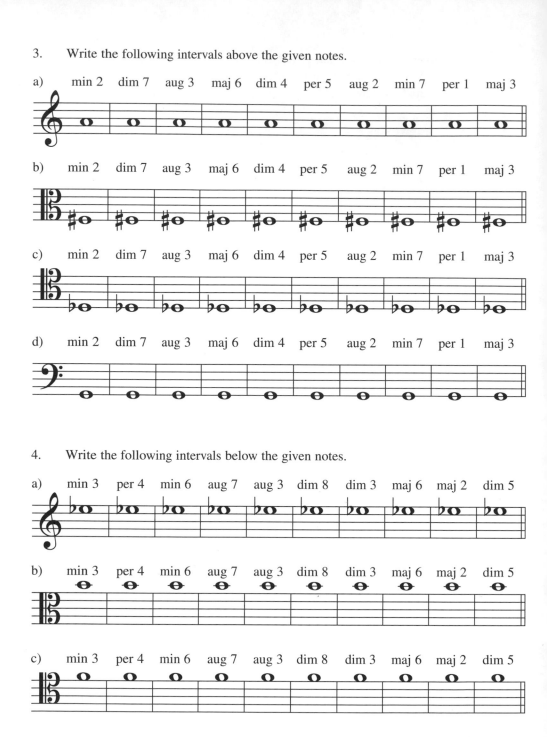

b) min 2 dim 7 aug 3 maj 6 dim 4 per 5 aug 2 min 7 per 1 maj 3

c) min 2 dim 7 aug 3 maj 6 dim 4 per 5 aug 2 min 7 per 1 maj 3

d) min 2 dim 7 aug 3 maj 6 dim 4 per 5 aug 2 min 7 per 1 maj 3

4. Write the following intervals below the given notes.

a) min 3 per 4 min 6 aug 7 aug 3 dim 8 dim 3 maj 6 maj 2 dim 5

b) min 3 per 4 min 6 aug 7 aug 3 dim 8 dim 3 maj 6 maj 2 dim 5

c) min 3 per 4 min 6 aug 7 aug 3 dim 8 dim 3 maj 6 maj 2 dim 5

d) min 3 per 4 min 6 aug 7 aug 3 dim 8 dim 3 maj 6 maj 2 dim 5

5. Name the following intervals. Invert them in the alto clef and name the inversions.

_____ _____ _____ _____ _____ _____ _____ _____ _____ _____

_____ _____ _____ _____ _____ _____ _____ _____ _____ _____

6. Name the following intervals. Invert them in the tenor clef and name the inversions.

_____ _____ _____ _____ _____ _____ _____ _____ _____ _____

_____ _____ _____ _____ _____ _____ _____ _____ _____ _____

7. Name the following intervals. Change the upper note of each enharmonically and rename the intervals.

_____ _____ _____ _____ _____

_____ _____ _____ _____ _____

8. Name the following intervals. Change the lower note of each enharmonically and rename the intervals.

9. Name the following compound intervals. Invert them and name the inversions.

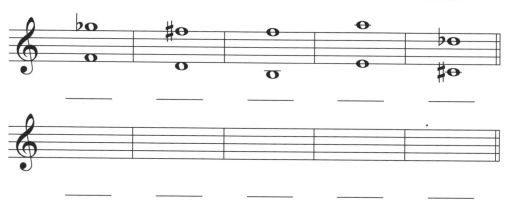

10. Name the following compound intervals. Invert them and name the inversions.

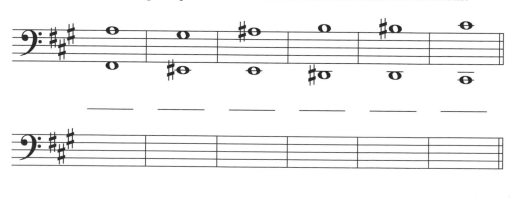

11. Name the following compound intervals. Invert them in the treble clef and name the inversions.

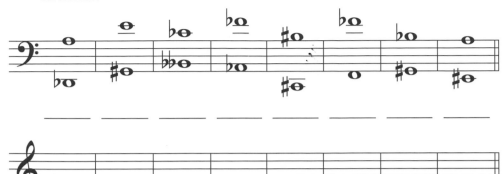

___ ___ ___ ___ ___ ___ ___

___ ___ ___ ___ ___ ___ ___

12. Name the following intervals.

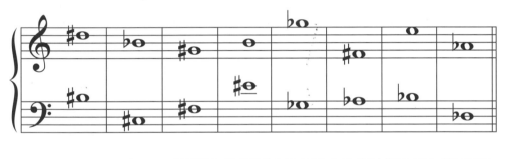

___ ___ ___ ___ ___ ___ ___

13. Name the intervals between successive notes of the following.

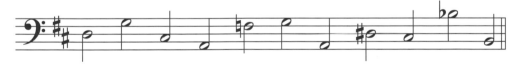

___ ___ ___ ___ ___ ___ ___ ___

14. Write three different major 3rds that are found in the scale of E♭ major.

15. Write three different major 6ths that are found in the scale of F minor, natural form.

16. Name all the scales (major, natural minor, and harmonic minor) in which each of these intervals may be found.

a)

b)

c)

17. Write a diminished 7th that is found in the scale of G harmonic minor.

18. Write three different perfect 4ths that are found in the scale of B major.

19. Write three different minor 2nds that are found in the scale of C♯ harmonic minor.

20. Write four different major 2nds that are found in the scale of A major.

21. Write the augmented 2nd that is found in the scale of G♯ harmonic minor.

22.   Write the augmented 5th that is found in the scale of B harmonic minor.

23.   Write four different minor 3rds that are found in the scale of E minor, natural form.

24.   Mark three major 3rds that occur between the different notes of this scale.

25.   Name all the scales (major, natural minor, and harmonic minor) in which each of the following intervals is found.

a)

_____

_____

_____

b)

_____

_____

_____

c)

_____

_____

_____

d)

_____

_____

_____

120

26. Mark all the perfect 4ths that occur between the different notes of this scale.

27. Name the following intervals. Name the one scale that contains them all.

Scale:

_____

_____ _____ _____ _____ _____

28. Name the following intervals. Name *two* scales that contain them all.

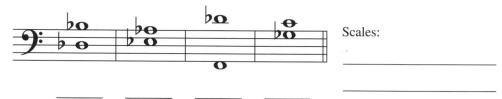

Scales:

_____

_____ _____ _____ _____

CHAPTER 5

CHORDS

TRIADS

P 1 2 1.   A CHORD is the name given to any three or more notes sounded simultaneously. The most basic chord is a TRIAD, that is, three sounds built up in 3rds.

Triads may be built on each degree of major and minor scales. The note that they are built on—that is, the lowest note—is called the ROOT of that triad. The next note is a diatonic 3rd above this root, and is named the THIRD, and the third sound is a diatonic 5th above the same root, and is called the FIFTH.

The triads built on the tonic, subdominant, and dominant scale degrees make up the group of chords known as PRIMARY TRIADS.

Here are the triads built on the tonic, subdominant, and dominant notes of the scale of D major.

D major

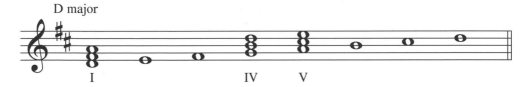

Note that chords are labeled with Roman numerals.

Here are the triads built on the tonic, subdominant, and dominant notes of the scale of G harmonic minor.

G minor (harmonic)

Note that only the harmonic form of the minor scale will be used for triads for the present. Therefore, the dominant triad in a minor key will need an accidental to raise the third of the chord, the leading note of the scale. (Triads built using the natural form of the minor scale will be covered later in this chapter.)

P 1 2   EXERCISES

1. Write the following triads in the treble clef, using the correct key signature for each.

   a) the dominant triad of A major

   b) the tonic triad of F major

   c) the subdominant triad of E♭ major

   d) the tonic triad of G major

   e) the dominant triad of E major

   f) the subdominant triad of D major

a)   b)   c)   d)   e)   f)

2. Write the following triads in the bass clef, using the correct key signature for each.

   a) the dominant triad of C minor

   b) the tonic triad of D minor

   c) the dominant triad of F♯ minor

   d) the subdominant triad of E minor

   e) the dominant triad of F minor

   f) the subdominant triad of C♯ minor

a)   b)   c)   d)   e)   f)

3. Write the following triads in the treble clef, using accidentals instead of a key signature.

   a) the tonic triad of B minor

   b) the dominant triad of C♯ minor

   c) the subdominant triad of F♯ minor

   d) the dominant triad of G minor

   e) the subdominant triad of A minor

   f) the dominant triad of D minor

   g) the tonic triad of C minor

   h) the dominant triad of E minor

a)   b)   c)   d)   e)   f)   g)   h)

4. Write the following triads in the bass clef, using accidentals instead of a key signature.

a) the tonic triad of A♭ major

b) the dominant triad of C major

c) the subdominant triad of B♭ major

d) the dominant triad of D major

e) the tonic triad of E♭ major

f) the subdominant triad of A major

g) the dominant triad of G major

h) the subdominant triad of E major

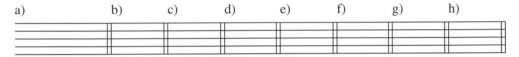

a)   b)   c)   d)   e)   f)   g)   h)

5. For each of the following, name the *major* key and identify the triad as tonic, subdominant, or dominant.

major key: ——— ——— ——— ——— ———

triad: ——— ——— ——— ——— ———

6. For each of the following, name the *minor* key and identify the triad as tonic, subdominant, or dominant.

minor key: ——— ——— ——— ——— ——— ———

triad: ——— ——— ——— ——— ——— ———

7. Fill in the blanks.

a) is the tonic triad of the key of _____.

b) is the dominant triad of the keys of _____ and _____.

c) is the subdominant triad of the key of _____.

d) is the tonic triad of the key of _____.

e) is the dominant triad of the keys of _____ and _____.

8. Fill in the blanks.

a) is the _____ triad in the key of _____.

b) is the _____ triad in the key of _____.

c) is the _____ triad in the key of _____.

d) is the _____ triad in the key of _____.

e) is the _____ triad in the key of _____.

1 2   2.   QUALITIES OF TRIADS: MAJOR AND MINOR

A MAJOR TRIAD has a major 3rd and a perfect 5th above the root.

Examples:

A MINOR TRIAD has a minor 3rd and a perfect 5th above the root.

Examples:

1 2   3.   Both major and minor triads occur in the major scale, built on different scale degrees. Here are the major and minor triads that occur in the scale of C major.

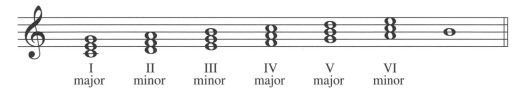

Both major and minor triads occur in the minor scale, built on different scale degrees. Here are the major and minor triads that occur in the scale of A harmonic minor.

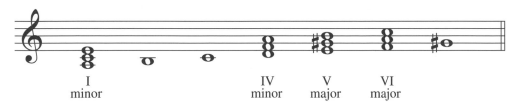

Triads not shown in the examples above have qualities other than major or minor and will be covered later in the chapter.

INVERSIONS

1 2   4.   A triad has two INVERSIONS. The first inversion has the third of the chord as the bottom note. The second inversion has the fifth of the chord as the bottom note.

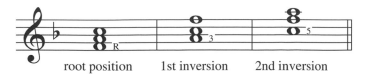

126

To SOLVE (that is, to identify) a triad, you must first put it in root position, and then you can tell its QUALITY and which POSITION it is in.

Example: Solve this triad.

When you put it in root position, it looks like this: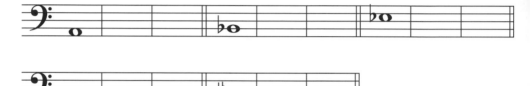

So the root is G, the quality of triad is minor, and the position is second inversion, since the 5th of the chord is on the bottom.

1 2 EXERCISES

1. Write a major triad and its inversions, using each of the following notes as the root.

2. Write a minor triad and its inversions, using each of the following notes as the root.

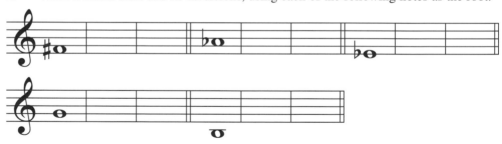

3. Solve the following triads.

root: ⎯⎯ ⎯⎯ ⎯⎯ ⎯⎯ ⎯⎯ ⎯⎯ ⎯⎯ ⎯⎯ ⎯⎯ ⎯⎯ ⎯⎯

quality: ⎯⎯ ⎯⎯ ⎯⎯ ⎯⎯ ⎯⎯ ⎯⎯ ⎯⎯ ⎯⎯ ⎯⎯ ⎯⎯ ⎯⎯

position: ⎯⎯ ⎯⎯ ⎯⎯ ⎯⎯ ⎯⎯ ⎯⎯ ⎯⎯ ⎯⎯ ⎯⎯ ⎯⎯ ⎯⎯

4. Write the following triads in the treble clef.

   a) the root position of the F major triad
   b) the root position of the D minor triad
   c) the first inversion of the G major triad
   d) the second inversion of the E minor triad
   e) the root position of the B♭ minor triad
   f) the second inversion of the C major triad
   g) the first inversion of the A♭ major triad
   h) the second inversion of the G♯ minor triad
   i) the root position of the B major triad
   j) the first inversion of the D major triad

a)   b)   c)   d)   e)

f)   g)   h)   i)   j)

5. Write the following triads in root position in the bass clef.

   a) a major triad with F as the root
   b) a minor triad with D as the fifth
   c) a minor triad with C as the third
   d) a major triad with G as the third
   e) a major triad with A♭ as the root
   f) a minor triad with A as the fifth
   g) a major triad with B as the fifth
   h) a minor triad with E♭ as the third
   i) a minor triad with B as the root
   j) a major triad with C♯ as the third

a)   b)   c)   d)   e)

f)   g)   h)   i)   j)

6.   Add accidentals where necessary to make each of these a major triad.

7.   Add accidentals where necessary to make each of these a minor triad.

8.   Write the following triads in the treble clef, using the correct key signature for each.

   a) the mediant triad of E♭ major, in root position

   b) the dominant triad of B♭ minor, in second inversion

   c) the tonic triad of E major, in first inversion

   d) the subdominant triad of F minor, in second inversion

   e) the supertonic triad of B major, in root position

a)   b)   c)   d)   e)

9.   Write the following triads in the bass clef, using the accidentals instead of key signatures.

   a) the tonic triad of A major, in first inversion

   b) the submediant triad of G♭ major, in root position

   c) the subdominant triad of C minor, in second inversion

   d) the dominant triad of F♯ minor, in first inversion

   e) the supertonic triad of B♭ major, in root position

a)   b)   c)   d)   e)

10. Identify the root, quality, and position of each of the following triads. Then name the major key of each and the technical degree of the root.

Example:

root: ___Ab___ _____ _____ _____ _____ _____

quality: __major__ _____ _____ _____ _____ _____

position: _2nd inv_ _____ _____ _____ _____ _____

major key: _Db maj_ _____ _____ _____ _____ _____

technical degree: _dominant_ _____ _____ _____ _____ _____

11. Identify the root, quality, and position of each of the following triads. Then name the minor key of each and the technical degree of the root.

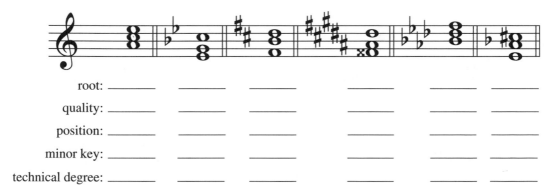

root: _____ _____ _____ _____ _____ _____

quality: _____ _____ _____ _____ _____ _____

position: _____ _____ _____ _____ _____ _____

minor key: _____ _____ _____ _____ _____ _____

technical degree: _____ _____ _____ _____ _____ _____

2 5. There are two other qualities of triads.

A DIMINISHED triad has a minor 3rd and a diminished 5th above the root.

An AUGMENTED triad has a major 3rd and an augmented 5th above the root.

2 6. All the triads in this chapter so far have been written in CLOSE position. They may also be written in OPEN position—that is, spread out over a distance of more than an octave. If one of the notes is doubled—meaning that it appears twice—the triad is in four-note form. The order in which the notes occur above the bottom note does not affect the position of the chord. It is always the lowest note that determines its position.

All of the following chords are different arrangements of the triad of C major in root position, and there are many more.

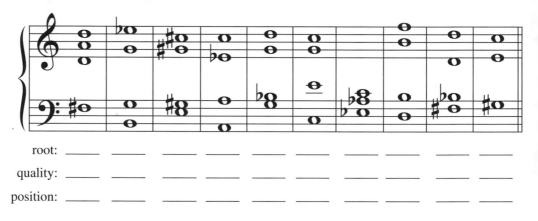

2 **EXERCISES**

1. Solve the following triads.

root: _____ _____ _____ _____ _____ _____ _____ _____ _____ _____

quality: _____ _____ _____ _____ _____ _____ _____ _____ _____ _____

position: _____ _____ _____ _____ _____ _____ _____ _____ _____ _____

2. Write the following triads in root position in the treble clef. Use close position.

a) an augmented triad with D as the third

b) a diminished triad with C♭ as the fifth

c) a diminished triad with C♯ as the root

d) an augmented triad with E♭ as the root

e) an augmented triad with D as the fifth

a)   b)   c)   d)   e)

3.   Write three different arrangements of each of the following triads in open position.

   a) the root position of the major triad of A♭

   b) the second inversion of the minor triad of F

   c) the first inversion of the minor triad of C

   d) the root position of the augmented triad of B

   e) the first inversion of the minor triad of F♯

   f) the second inversion of the diminished triad of E

   g) the first inversion of the augmented triad of A

   h) the root position of the diminished triad of C♯

   i) the second inversion of the major triad of D♭

   j) the first inversion of the minor triad of G

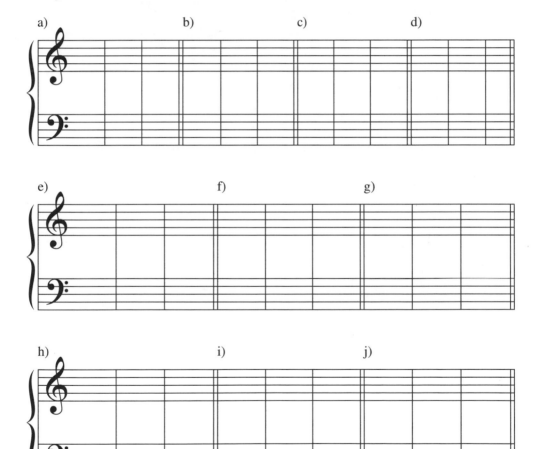

4. Write the four different kinds of triads in root position *below* each of the following notes.

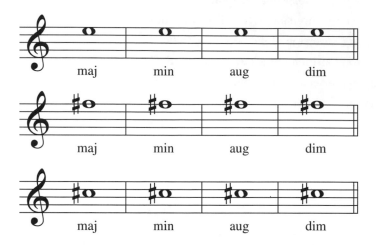

5. Write the four different kinds of triads in root position *above* each of the following notes.

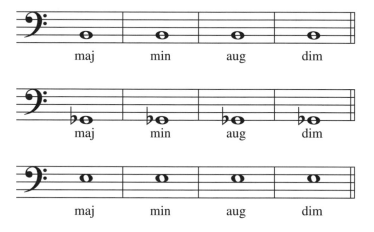

2 7.   IDENTIFYING THE SCALES IN WHICH A GIVEN TRIAD IS FOUND

You can see from the following examples that every major scale has a major triad on the tonic, subdominant, and dominant; a minor triad on the supertonic, mediant, and submediant; and a diminished triad on the leading note.

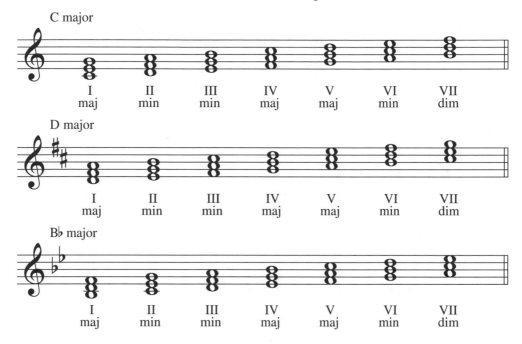

Harmonic minor scales have major triads on the dominant and submediant; minor triads on the tonic and subdominant; diminished triads on the supertonic and leading note; and an augmented triad on the mediant.

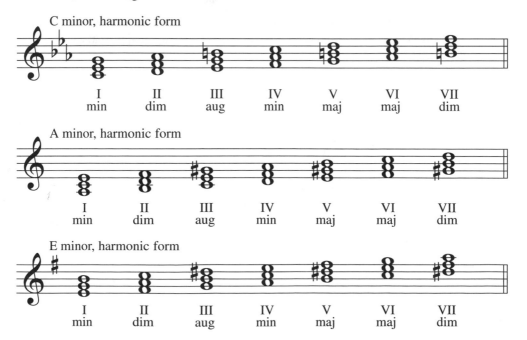

134

Natural minor scales have major triads on the mediant, submediant, and subtonic; minor triads on the tonic, subdominant, and dominant; and a diminished triad on the supertonic.

C minor, natural form

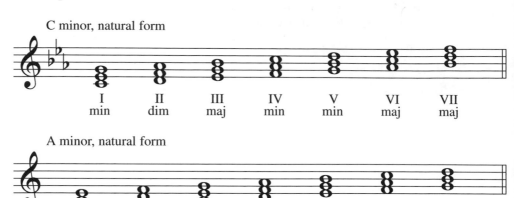

Note that the I, II, IV, and VI triads are the same in the harmonic and natural forms of the minor scale, since these four triads do not contain the seventh scale degree. The III, V, and VII triads do contain the seventh scale degree, so these triads have different qualities in the harmonic and natural minor scales.

Since there are eight different places where a major triad can occur in the major, harmonic minor, and natural minor scales, then any major triad can be found in eight different scales.

Example 1

The root, F, of this major triad can be the tonic, subdominant, and dominant note of major scales containing F, A, and C. Therefore, this triad is found in the F major, C major, and B♭ major scales. Also, F is the dominant and submediant note of the harmonic minor scales containing F, A, and C, namely B♭ and A harmonic minor. Finally, F is the mediant, submediant, and subtonic of the natural minor scales containing F, A, C; namely D, A, and G minor, natural form.

Remember to count *down* from the root of the triad to find the tonic.

A good way to say it is: If F is I, then I is F major

If F is IV, then I is C major

If F is V, then I is B♭ major, and so on.

Example 2

There are also eight places where minor triads occur: on II, III, and VI of major scales, on I and IV of harmonic minor scales, and on I, IV, and V of natural minor scales. The triad shown on the left is found in C, B♭, and F major scales, in D and A harmonic minor scales, and in D, A, and G natural minor scales.

Example 3

There are four places where diminished triads are found: on VII of the major scale, on II and VII of the harmonic minor scale, and on II of the natural minor scale. The following triad is found in the F major scale, in the D and F harmonic minor scales, and in the D natural minor scale.

Example 4

The augmented triad is found only on III of a harmonic minor scale. The only scale in which this chord can be found is E harmonic minor.

Here is a chart to summarize the scale degrees on which the triads are found.

	Major Scales	Harmonic Minor Scales	Natural Minor Scales
major triads	I IV V	V VI	III VI VII
minor triads	II III VI	I IV	I IV V
diminished triads	VII	II VII	II
augmented triads	none	III	none

2   EXERCISES

1.   Write and name all the triads found in the A major scale.

I   II   III   IV   V   VI   VII

quality: _____   _____   _____   _____   _____   _____   _____

2.   Write and name all the triads found in the E♭ major scale.

I	II	III	IV	V	VI	VII

quality: _____ _____ _____ _____ _____ _____ _____

3.   (a) Write and name all the triads found in the F minor scale, harmonic form.

I	II	III	IV	V	VI	VII

quality: _____ _____ _____ _____ _____ _____ _____

      (b) Write and name all the triads found in the F minor scale, natural form.

I	II	III	IV	V	VI	VII

quality: _____ _____ _____ _____ _____ _____ _____

4.   (a) Write and name all the triads found in the G minor scale, harmonic form.

I	II	III	IV	V	VI	VII

quality: _____ _____ _____ _____ _____ _____ _____

      (b) Write and name all the triads found in the G minor scale, natural form.

I	II	III	IV	V	VI	VII

quality: _____ _____ _____ _____ _____ _____ _____

5. Name all the scales (major, harmonic minor, and natural minor) in which each of the following triads is found.

(a)

(b)

(c)

(d)

6. Write the triad that is found only in the G minor harmonic scale.

7. Write the triad that is common only to these scales: B♭ major, G minor (harmonic and natural forms), and B♭ minor (harmonic form only).

8. Name all the scales (major, harmonic minor, and natural minor) in which each of the following triads is found.

(a)

(b)

9.   Write the triad that is common only to these scales: D♭ major, B♭ minor (harmonic and natural forms), G♭ major, F minor (harmonic and natural forms), A♭ major, and E♭ minor (natural form only).

10. In the treble clef, write the diminished triads that are found in the following scales:
     a) D major b) A♭ major c) B major d) E major e) D♭ major

a)   b)   c)   d)   e)

11. In the bass clef, write the augmented triads that are found in the following harmonic minor scales: a) B minor b) G♯ minor c) C minor d) F minor e) D minor

a)   b)   c)   d)   e)

12. Write the following triads in close position in the treble clef, using the proper key signature for each. Name the quality of each triad.

     a) the mediant triad of F minor, natural form, in root position
     b) the leading-note triad of G♯ minor, harmonic form, in second inversion
     c) the subdominant triad of E minor, in first inversion
     d) the dominant triad of B♭ minor, natural form, in first inversion
     e) the tonic triad of A♭ minor, in second inversion
     f) the mediant triad of C minor, harmonic form, in first inversion
     g) the subtonic triad of C♯ minor, natural form, in second inversion
     h) the dominant triad of D♯ minor, harmonic form, in root position

a)   b)   c)   d)

quality: _____   _____   _____   _____

e)   f)   g)   h)

quality: _____   _____   _____   _____

     Why was the form (harmonic or natural) of the minor scale to be used in parts c) and e) not specified?
     _____

     _____

13. Write the following triads in close position in the bass clef, using accidentals instead of key signatures. Name the quality of each triad.

   a) the supertonic triad of F major, in root position

   b) the dominant triad of B♭ minor, harmonic form, in first inversion

   c) the tonic triad of F♯ minor, in first inversion

   d) the subtonic triad of G minor, natural form, in second inversion

   e) the mediant triad of E♭ major, in root position

   f) the submediant triad of B major, in first inversion

   g) the subdominant triad of C minor, in second inversion

   h) the dominant triad of G♯ minor, natural form, in root position

   i) the tonic triad of C♯ major, in first inversion

   j) the supertonic triad of D minor, in second inversion

a)　　　　　　b)　　　　　c)　　　　　d)　　　　　e)

quality: _____   _____   _____   _____   _____

f)　　　　　　g)　　　　　h)　　　　　i)　　　　　j)

quality: _____   _____   _____   _____   _____

DOMINANT SEVENTH CHORDS

2 8. Here is the dominant TRIAD of C major.

Here is the dominant SEVENTH CHORD of C major.

You can see that another diatonic 3rd has been added above the dominant triad, giving a root, a major 3rd, a perfect 5th, and a minor 7th.

Here is the dominant 7th chord of C minor.

Its *sound* is identical to the dominant 7th of its *tonic* major, but the notation is different, as the minor key has a different key signature, and therefore an accidental is required to raise the leading note, which is the third of the chord. Only the harmonic form of the minor scale will be used for dominant 7th chords.

2   9.   INVERSIONS

A dominant 7th chord has three inversions.

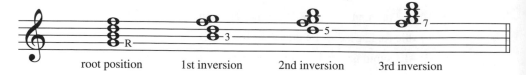

root position   1st inversion   2nd inversion   3rd inversion

- When the root is on the bottom, the chord is in root position.
- When the third is on the bottom, the chord is in first inversion.
- When the fifth is on the bottom, the chord is in second inversion.
- When the seventh is on the bottom, the chord is in third inversion.

As in triads, only the bottom note determines the position, and the arrangements of the notes above it can vary.

These are all arrangements of the second inversion of the dominant 7th of C major.

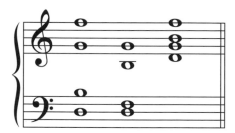

2   10.   When solving a dominant 7th chord, rearrange the notes into close and root position first, then find the root, the key, and the position.

Rearrange this: 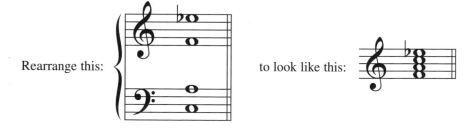 to look like this:

Then we know that F is the root. Therefore, F is the dominant of the key, B♭. Since the fifth of the chord is on the bottom, the chord is in second inversion.

So the complete answer is:

root: F

key: B♭ major or B♭ minor

position: 2nd inversion

11. Note that, depending on how a dominant 7th chord is notated, there may be either one or two correct answers for the name of its key.

If the dominant 7th chord is written using a key signature, then there will be only one correct key name.

Example 1

- The key signature of two sharps implies D major or B minor.
- The root of the dominant 7th chord is A.
- Since A is V of D, the key must be D major.

Example 2

- The key signature implies D major or B minor.
- The root of the dominant 7th chord is F♯.
- Since F♯ is V of B, the key must be B minor.

If the dominant 7th chord is written using accidentals instead of a key signature, then it can belong to two keys. The two keys will be tonic major and minor.

Example 3

- There is no key signature.
- The root of the dominant 7th chord is D.
- D is V of G; the keys are G major and minor.

2   12.   You may be asked to work a question similar to this:

Write the dominant 7th chord, and inversions of other dominant 7ths, using D as the lowest note in each case. Name the major key of each.

The answer will have four different dominant 7ths, in four different major keys. D will be the root of the first chord, the third of the second chord, the fifth of the third, and the seventh of the last chord.

a)   The root position has D as the root. Therefore, the key is G major.

b)   Since D is the third, B♭ is the root, and the key is E♭ major.

c)   Since D is the fifth, G is the root, and the key is C major.

d)   Since D is the seventh, E is the root, and the key is A major.

2   **EXERCISES**

1.   Write the dominant 7th chord and its inversions in each of the following keys, using the correct key signature for each.

a)   A major

b)   E♭ major

c)   B minor

d)   F minor

e)   C♯ minor

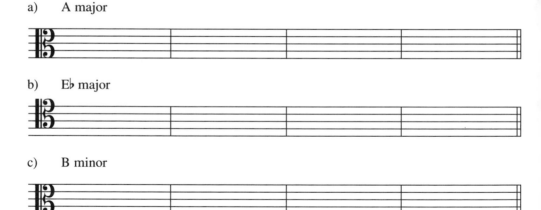

f)   B♭ major

g)   G♯ minor

h)   D major

i)   E minor

2.   Solve the following dominant 7th chords.

a)   b)   c)   d)   e)

root: _____   _____   _____   _____   _____

key 1:   _____   _____   _____   _____   _____

key 2:   _____   _____   _____   _____   _____

position: _____   _____   _____   _____   _____

f)   g)   h)   i)   j)

root: _____   _____   _____   _____   _____

key 1:   _____   _____   _____   _____   _____

key 2:   _____   _____   _____   _____   _____

position: _____   _____   _____   _____   _____

3. Write the following dominant 7ths in the treble clef, using the correct key signature for each.

   a) the first inversion of the dominant 7th of D minor

   b) the second inversion of the dominant 7th of F♯ minor

   c) the root position of the dominant 7th of B major

   d) the third inversion of the dominant 7th of G minor

   e) the root position of the dominant 7th of E♭ major

   f) the first inversion of the dominant 7th of C♯ minor

   g) the second inversion of the dominant 7th of A major

   h) the root position of the dominant 7th of G♭ major

   i) the third inversion of the dominant 7th of G♯ minor

   j) the second inversion of the dominant 7th of D♭ major

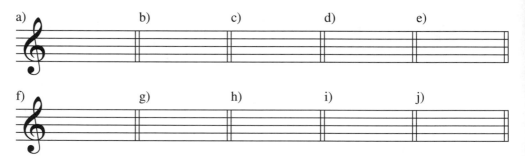

4. Write the dominant 7th, and inversions of other dominant 7ths, using F as the lowest note in each case. Name the major key of each.

             root position   1st inversion   2nd inversion   3rd inversion

key: _____   _____   _____   _____

5. Add accidentals to the following to make them into dominant 7th chords. Name the minor key of each.

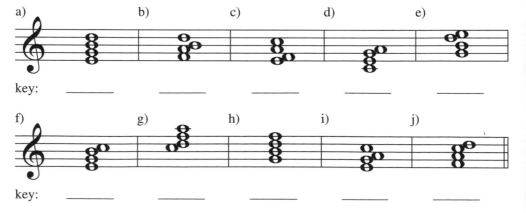

key: _____   _____   _____   _____   _____

key: _____   _____   _____   _____   _____

6. Solve the following dominant 7th chords.

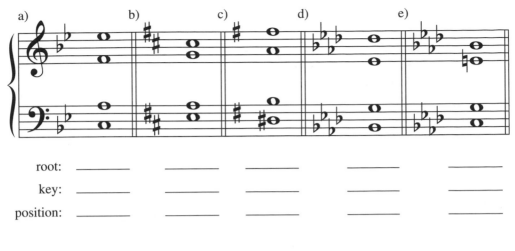

root: _____ _____ _____ _____ _____

key: _____ _____ _____ _____ _____

position: _____ _____ _____ _____ _____

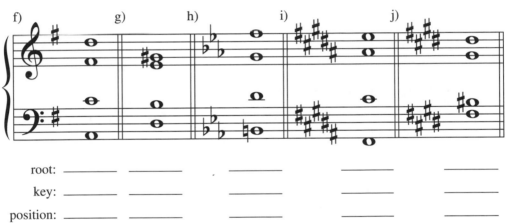

root: _____ _____ _____ _____ _____

key: _____ _____ _____ _____ _____

position: _____ _____ _____ _____ _____

7. Write the dominant 7th and inversions of other dominant 7ths, using E as the lowest note for each. Name two keys for each.

	root position	1st inversion	2nd inversion	3rd inversion
key 1:	_____	_____	_____	_____
key 2:	_____	_____	_____	_____

8. Write the dominant 7th and inversions of other dominant 7ths, using G as the lowest note for each. Name the minor key of each.

root position   1st inversion   2nd inversion   3rd inversion

key: _____   _____   _____   _____

9. Write the dominant 7th and inversions of other dominant 7ths, using A as the lowest note of each. Name two keys for each.

root position   1st inversion   2nd inversion   3rd inversion

key 1: _____   _____   _____   _____

key 2: _____   _____   _____   _____

SUMMARY OF CHORD TYPES

So far, we have studied two different types of chords: triads and seventh chords. Here is a brief review.

2 13. TRIADS

A triad is a chord consisting of a root, a third, and a fifth. We have seen that there are four qualities of triads. The quality is determined by the specific size of each interval in the triad.

- A major triad consists of a root, a major 3rd, and a perfect 5th.
- A minor triad consists of a root, a minor 3rd, and a perfect 5th.
- A diminished triad consists of a root, a minor 3rd, and a diminished 5th.
- An augmented triad consists of a root, a major 3rd, and an augmented 5th.

2 14. SEVENTH CHORDS

A seventh chord is a chord consisting of a root, a third, a fifth, and a seventh. We have studied one kind of seventh chord, the dominant 7th. It has a root, a major 3rd, a perfect 5th, and a minor 7th.

Opt.   There are many other qualities of seventh chords. The most common qualities are the following:

- major 7th chord (root, major 3rd, perfect 5th, major 7th)
- minor 7th chord (root, minor 3rd, perfect 5th, minor 7th)
- diminished 7th chord (root, minor 3rd, diminished 5th, diminished 7th)
- half-diminished 7th chord (root, minor 3rd, diminished 5th, minor 7th)

Both triads and seventh chords are built using notes which are a 3rd apart. Chords based on other intervals have become widely used since the beginning of the 20th century. Some additional chord types are described below.

OTHER CHORD TYPES

2   15.   QUARTAL CHORDS

A quartal chord is a chord built on a series of 4ths. A quartal chord may have three or more notes. The quality of the 4ths may vary (e.g., perfect 4ths, augmented 4ths). These are all quartal chords:

Examples

2   16.   POLYCHORDS

A polychord is a combination of two or more different chords. The component chords are often placed in widely separate registers or played by different instruments, so they may be clearly perceived by the listener as different chords.

Examples

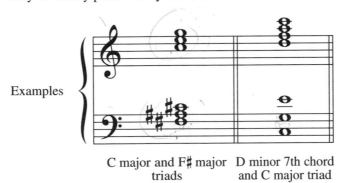

C major and F♯ major   D minor 7th chord
triads   and C major triad

2   17.   CLUSTERS

A cluster is a chord consisting of at least three adjacent notes of a scale. The number of notes and the type of scale on which the cluster is based may vary. In some cases, graphic notation is used to indicate a cluster.

Examples

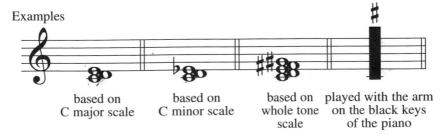

based on   based on   based on   played with the arm
C major scale   C minor scale   whole tone   on the black keys
                                  scale   of the piano

148

2 EXERCISES

1. Name each of the following chords as: triad, seventh chord, quartal chord, polychord, or cluster. For the triads, also state the quality. Indicate any seventh chords that are dominant 7ths as "V^7." Triads and seventh chords may appear in root position or in any inversion.

Example:

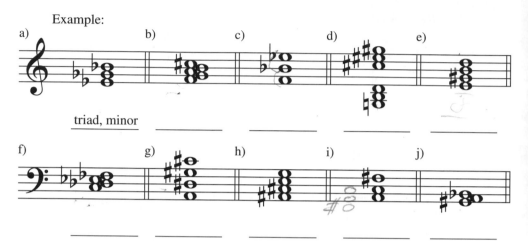

triad, minor _____ _____ _____ _____

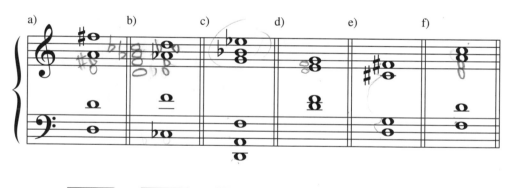

_____ _____ _____ _____ _____

2. See instructions for Exercise 1.

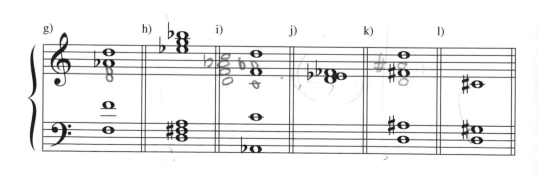

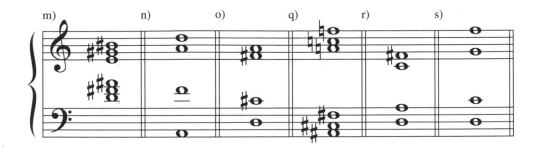

3.   See instructions for Exercise 1.

MORE ABOUT CHORD SYMBOLS

Opt.   18.   ROMAN NUMERALS AND QUALITIES OF CHORDS

Many harmony textbooks use a more detailed system of chord symbols than the one used in this book. The Roman numerals that are used to label triads may be written so as to indicate the qualities of triads.

- In this system, a major triad is labeled with an upper-case Roman numeral (examples: I, IV, etc.).

- A minor triad is labeled with a lower-case Roman numeral (examples: i, iv, etc.).

- A diminished triad is labeled with a lower-case Roman numeral followed by a degree sign ° (examples: ii°, vii°).

- An augmented triad is labeled with an upper-case Roman numeral followed by either an × or a + sign (examples: III×, III+).

- The dominant 7th chord is labeled with an upper-case Roman numeral V followed by an arabic numeral ^{7}: V^7.

Opt.   19.   POPULAR CHORD SYMBOLS

Popular chord symbols identify a chord by its root, quality, and sometimes, its bass note. Unlike Roman numerals, popular chord symbols do not indicate how a chord functions in a particular key.

The *root* of the chord is named using a capital (upper-case) letter. Any accidental that affects the root must be included in the chord symbol.

The *qualities* of triads are indicated as follows.

- A major triad is simply identified by the name of its root.

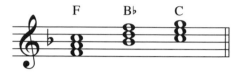

- A minor triad is identified by the name of its root followed by a lower case "m."

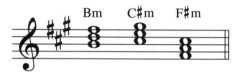

- A diminished triad is identified by the name of its root followed by "dim."

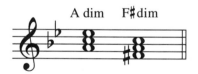

Alternatively, the ° sign may be used (A°, F♯°).

- An augmented triad is identified by the name of its root followed by a + sign.

Alternatively, an ˣ sign or "aug" may be used (Dˣ, D aug).

A dominant 7th chord is identified by the name of its root followed by the arabic numeral [7].

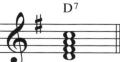

The *position* of a chord may also be specified. Root position chords simply use the chord symbols outlined above. An inverted chord is indicated by writing the root-quality symbol over the name of the bass note.

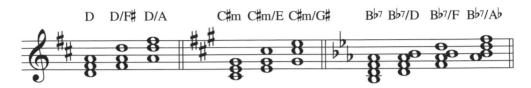

Opt. EXERCISES

1. Write the following scales in the treble clef, ascending only, using key signatures. Use whole notes. Build a triad on each scale degree. Label the triads with Roman numerals that indicate the qualities of the chords.

a) D major

b) G minor, harmonic form

c) E minor, natural form

2. Write the popular chord symbol for each of the following.

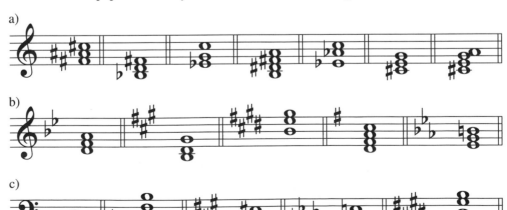

CHAPTER 6

CADENCES AND MELODY WRITING

CADENCE TYPES

1 2 1. A CADENCE is a two-chord formula that marks the end of every phrase of classical music, thereby providing a type of musical punctuation. The second of these chords is nearly always on an accented beat. You will learn about the many forms of cadences in detail when you begin to study harmony. It is important that you play these cadences as you study them, so that you will be able to recognize them by sound as well as by sight.

For present purposes, we will write cadences in KEYBOARD STYLE. The root of each chord will be put in the bass, and the three notes of the triad will be in close position in the treble clef, in any one of the three positions depending on which note you want in the melody.

Remember: it is the note in the bass—not the lowest note in the treble clef—that determines the position of the chord. Therefore, these cadences will all be in root position.

1 2 2. There are two kinds of cadences, which may be classified as "final" and "non-final."

The two types of "final" cadences which may be found at the end of a phrase or at the end of a piece of music are the PERFECT CADENCE and the PLAGAL CADENCE.

1 2 3. The PERFECT CADENCE is the most common of all cadences. It is also called an authentic cadence. It consists of the dominant chord followed by the tonic chord (or V–I). Here are some examples of perfect cadences.

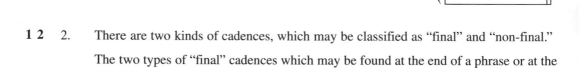

C major: V I   D major: V I   G minor: V I   B♭ major: V I

1 2 4. **CADENCES IN MINOR KEYS**

In Chapter 5, we studied triads built using both the harmonic and the natural forms of the minor scale. The minor dominant triad found in the natural minor scale is not used in the cadences covered here. Use the harmonic form of the minor scale for all cadences in minor keys; the leading note must be raised and the dominant triad must be major in quality.

1 2 5. The PLAGAL CADENCE is the other kind of cadence that sounds "final." It consists of the subdominant chord followed by the tonic chord. It is often found added to the end of a piece, after a perfect cadence, like an Amen after a hymn.

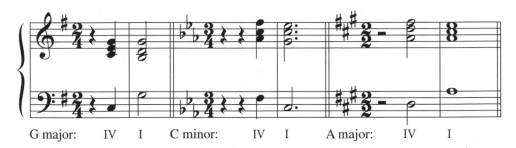

G major: IV   I   C minor: IV   I   A major: IV   I

1 2 6. **HOW TO WRITE CADENCES**

In writing cadences, it is very important to make the movement between the two chords as smooth as possible, avoiding all unnecessary leaps. Therefore, the following procedure is advisable at this stage.

1 2 7. To write a perfect cadence, V–I:

1. Write the dominant note in the bass clef, followed by the tonic note.

2. Select any one of the notes of the dominant triad to be the melody note and write it in the treble clef above the dominant bass note. Then write the other two notes of the dominant triad below it in close position. None of these notes may be lower than the bass note.

3. Write the three notes of the tonic triad in the treble clef above the tonic bass note, joining them to the notes of the dominant triad as follows:

   • Keep the common note* in the same voice part.
   • Move the other two notes *up* a 2nd.

C major

* A common note is one that appears in both triads. Example: In the key of C major, G is the common note between the dominant triad G–B–D and the tonic triad C–E–G.

Remember that because the dominant triad contains the leading note, it will require an accidental in the minor key.

Since there can be three different melody notes, there can be three different forms of perfect cadences when this procedure is followed.

C major

In all exercises, be sure to complete the time of each measure with rests.

Frequently, the last two notes of a melody will move down from the supertonic to the tonic. In this case, the above rules obviously cannot apply. The notes of the dominant triad will all have to move *down* to the nearest available note of the tonic triad. The common note will not remain in the same voice part. This is another way of writing a perfect cadence which is quite acceptable and often used.

G major

1 2   8.   To write a plagal cadence, IV–I, follow the same general procedure as for the perfect cadence.

1. Write the subdominant note in the bass clef, followed by the tonic note.

2. Write the three notes of the subdominant triad in the treble clef above the subdominant bass note, selecting one to be the melody note.

3. Write the three notes of the tonic triad in the treble clef above the tonic bass note, joining them to the notes of the subdominant triad by keeping the common note in the same voice part, and moving the other two notes down a 2nd.

A major

1 2 EXERCISES

1. Identify the key and the kind of cadence for each of the following.

key: _____ _____ _____

cadence: _____ _____ _____

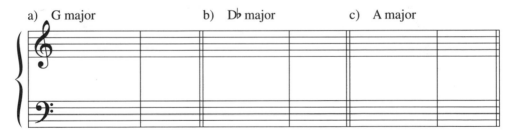

key: _____ _____

cadence: _____ _____

2. Write a two-measure example of a perfect cadence in each of the following keys. Use $\frac{3}{4}$ time.

a) G major   b) D♭ major   c) A major

d) C minor   e) F minor

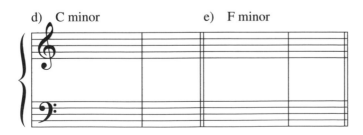

3.   Write a two-measure example of a plagal cadence in each of the following keys. Use $\frac{2}{2}$ time.

a)   A♭ major   b)   B minor   c)   F minor

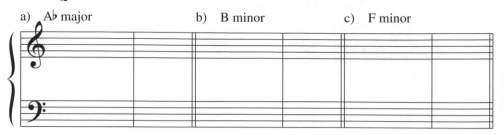

d)   E minor   e)   E major

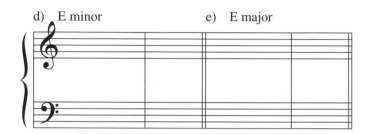

4.   The following are melody notes of either perfect or plagal cadences. Complete the cadences and name the type of each.

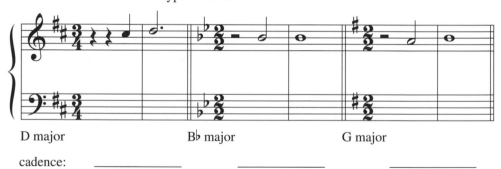

D major   B♭ major   G major

cadence: _____   _____   _____

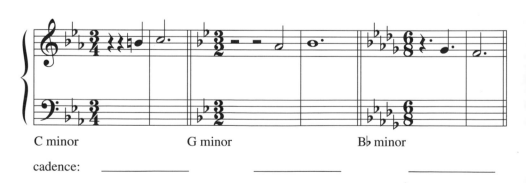

C minor   G minor   B♭ minor

cadence: _____   _____   _____

2 9. A non-final cadence, which occurs in the *middle* of a composition, is the IMPERFECT CADENCE. The second chord of this cadence is always the dominant, but the first chord can be one of several. The ones we will use here to approach the dominant are the tonic and the subdominant (I–V or IV–V).

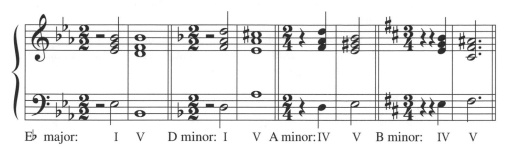

E♭ major: I   V   D minor: I   V A minor:IV   V B minor: IV   V

2 10. To write an imperfect cadence, I–V, reverse the procedure used for writing the perfect cadence.

1. Write the tonic note followed by the dominant note in the bass clef.

2. Write the three notes of the tonic triad above the tonic bass note.

3. Write the three notes of the dominant triad above the dominant bass note, joining them to the first triad by keeping the common note in the same voice part, and moving the remaining two notes *down* a 2nd.

G minor

If the melody notes move up from the tonic to the supertonic, then the above rules cannot apply. In this case, reverse the procedure for writing a perfect cadence with the melody moving from the supertonic to the tonic. The notes of the tonic triad will all have to move *up* to the nearest notes of the dominant triad.

G minor

2   10.   To write an imperfect cadence, IV–V:

1. Write the subdominant note in the bass clef, and move it up a 2nd to the dominant note.

2. Write the notes of the subdominant triad in the treble clef above the subdominant bass note.

3. Move all three notes of the subdominant triad *down* to the *nearest* note of the dominant triad. You will find that one note will fall a 3rd, and the other two notes will fall a 2nd. Note that there is no common note between these two chords.

G major

Contrary motion between the bass and the right-hand chord is an essential characteristic of the IV–V imperfect cadence. Do not let the right hand move in the same direction as the bass. Also, do not let the bass jump down a 7th.

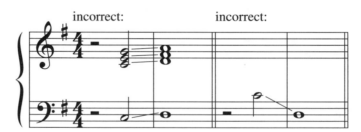

2   EXERCISES

1.   For each of the following, name the key, write the Roman numeral for each chord, and name the cadence.

_____   __ __ __   _____   __ __

_____   _____   _____

_____   _____   _____

_____   _____   _____

_____   __ __ __   __ __ __

_____   _____   _____

2 2. Write two different examples of imperfect cadences in each of the following keys. Use $\frac{2}{2}$ time.

a) D major

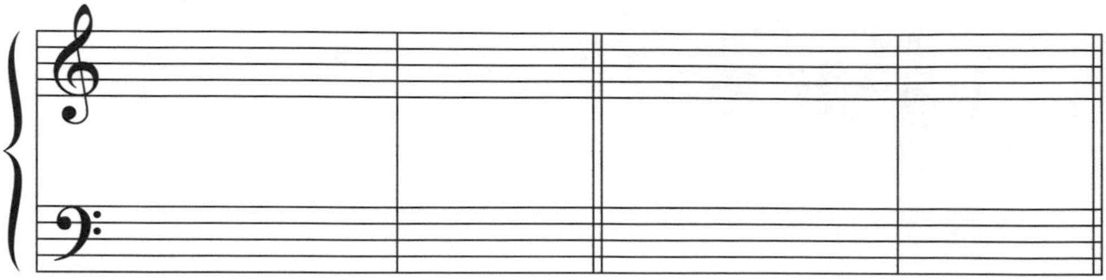

b) B♭ minor

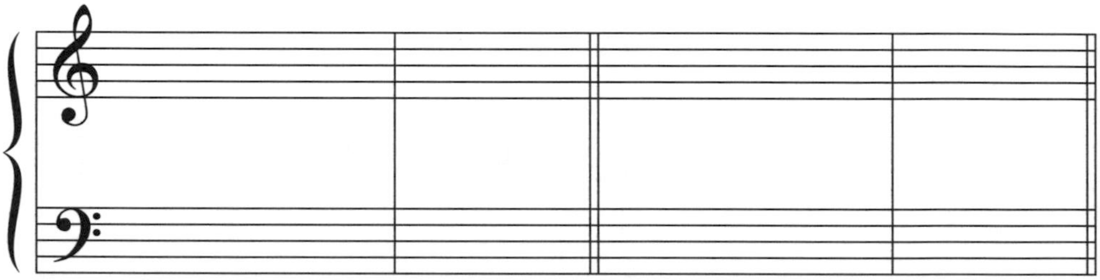

c) G♯ minor

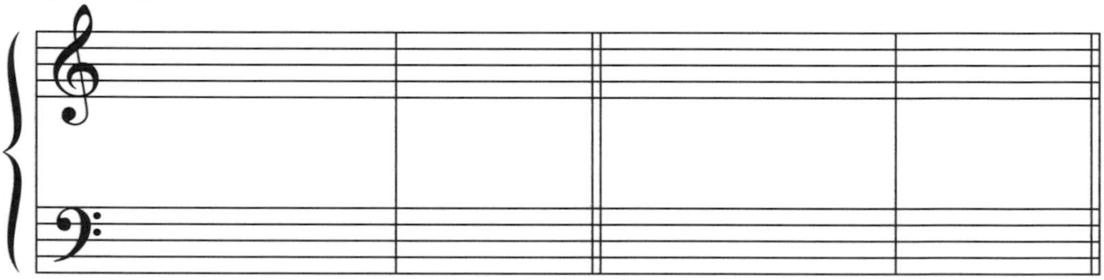

d) A♭ major

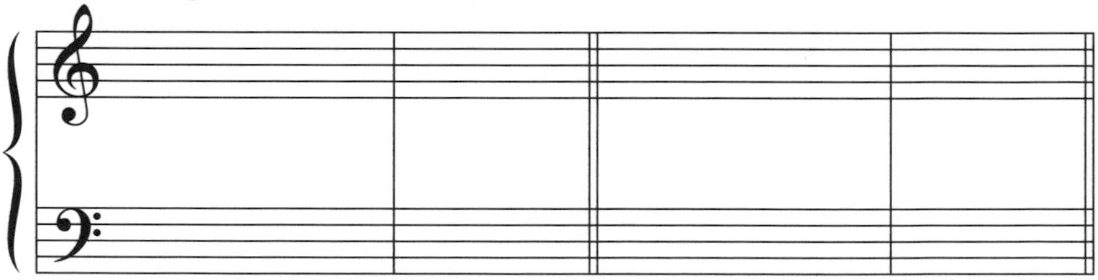

e) C minor

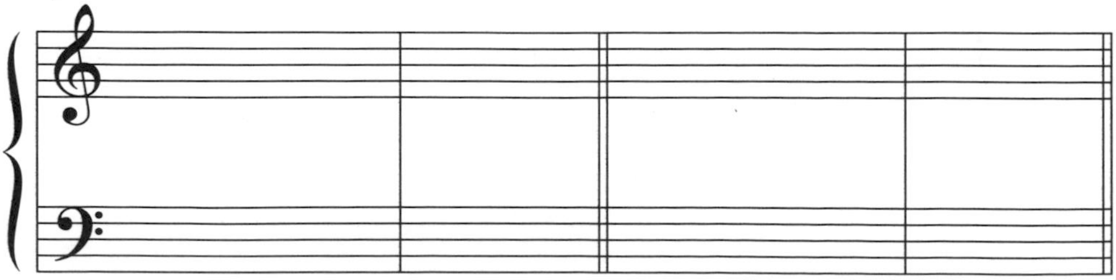

f) C# minor

g) B major

3. Write a two-measure example of each of the three kinds of cadences in each of the following keys. Use $\frac{3}{2}$ time.

a) A major

b) G minor

c) E minor

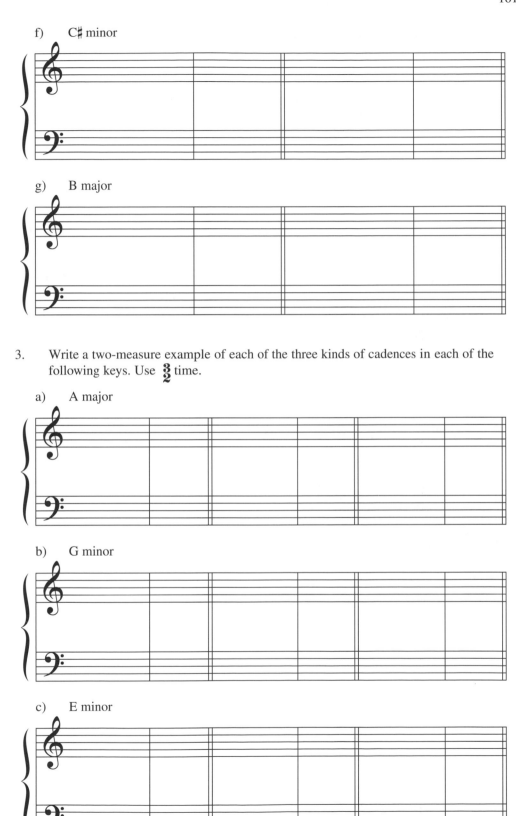

4. The following are the melody notes of perfect, plagal, or imperfect cadences. Complete the cadences and name the type of each.

B major _____   D major _____   E♭ major _____

F major _____   D minor _____   C minor _____

INSERTING CADENCES IN A TWO-PHRASE MELODY

P 2   12.   A cadence is found on the last two notes of each phrase.

Question: Write a cadence at the end of each phrase of the following melody, and name each cadence used.

Method:

1. Find the key of the melody.

2. Write down the letter names of the triads on I, IV, and V in that key.

3. By looking at the last two melody notes of the first phrase, decide which kind of cadence will fit, remembering that an imperfect cadence usually occurs in the middle of a piece, and a final cadence at then end.

4. In the bass clef, write the root of each of the two cadential chords under the last two notes of the phrase.

key: G minor

I	G	B♭	D
IV	C	E♭	G
V	D	F♯	A

IV V

5. In the treble clef, write the missing notes of each triad below the given melody notes, joining the stems to the given melody notes.

6. If the melody is in a minor key, raise the leading note in the dominant triad.

7. Add rests to complete the time in the bass for the measures containing the cadence.

8. Name the cadence as perfect, plagal, or imperfect.

9. By looking at the last two melody notes of the second phrase, decide on either perfect or plagal for the final cadence.

10. Repeat steps 4 to 8.

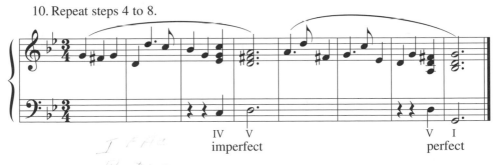

IV V
imperfect

V I
perfect

2 EXERCISES

1. Name the key of each of the following melodies. Write a cadence at the end of each phrase, and name each cadence.

a)

MELODY WRITING WITH CADENCES

2 13. We will begin the study of melody writing by creating a response to a given melodic opening. As in the preceding exercises, the cadence at the end of each melodic phrase is to be harmonized.

Many melodies consist of two phrases that create the effect of "question and answer."

Most phrases are four measures long. Other phrase lengths are possible but are far less common, and we will not use them here. In a two-phrase "question and answer" melody, a four-measure phrase is answered by a four-measure phrase, creating a melody that is eight measures long.

Phrase 1

The first phrase will be given in each exercise. Most often, the "question" phrase ends with an imperfect cadence. Occasionally, a perfect cadence may occur here; very rarely a plagal cadence. While the melody will be given in phrase 1, you will need to harmonize the cadence.

Be careful when naming the key of the melody. Since the end of the melody is not given, you cannot depend on the final note as a guide to the key. If you name the key incorrectly, your cadences and answering phrase will not work.

Suggestion: Study the section of Chapter 8 that deals with naming the key of a given melody. (See pp. 206–213.)

Phrase 2

The answering phrase that you write must work together with the given phrase to create a unified and complete melody.

For these exercises, each melody should end with a perfect cadence. The end of the melody will sound strongest and most final if it stops on the tonic note. For now, avoid ending on any other scale degree.

Since you will have to harmonize the cadence at the end of your melody, it is best to approach the final tonic *by step,* either from above (supertonic to tonic) or from below (leading note to tonic). Avoid ending with a leap to the tonic note; your melody could be fine, but it would be difficult to connect the chords smoothly when writing the cadence.

If the opening phrase begins with an upbeat, then your response should begin with an upbeat of the same time value. Remember to deduct the duration of the upbeat from the final measure.

In melody writing, there is never one single correct answer, or even a "best" answer. Any opening phrase can be answered in many different ways. As you begin melody writing, it is best to let your answering phrase resemble the given phrase very closely. Do not hesitate to repeat most of phrase 1 to create phrase 2; remember that the end of the phrase will have to be altered to create a strong, final-sounding perfect cadence.

An answering phrase may also vary the "question" phrase in a number of ways, or it may even contrast with the opening phrase. Study the following examples, which show several different answers to each given opening.

Example 1

key: _____   _____

answer 1(a)

key: ___C major___   ___imperfect___

___perfect___

The given phrase has been repeated almost entirely. Only the last two notes have been changed.

The melody ends on the tonic note. The tonic is approached by step from the leading note.

Both the opening phrase and the answering phrase start with a one-beat upbeat. The final measure, therefore, has only two beats.

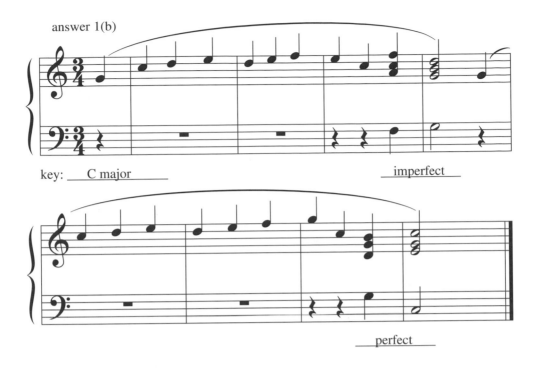

Like answer 1(a), answer 1(b) begins by repeating the given phrase.

In 1(b), the end of the phrase has been altered not only to end on $\hat{1}$, but also to introduce a new high point into the melodic line.

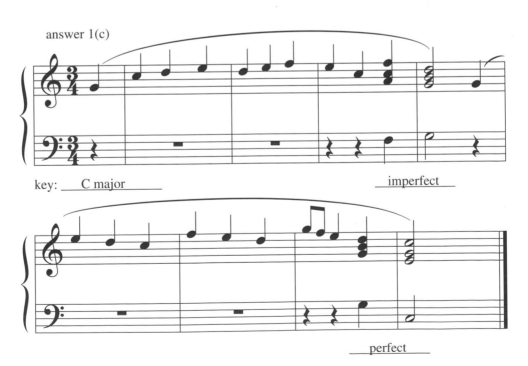

Answer 1(c) is clearly based on the given phrase, but avoids literal repetition of it.

In m. 5, the melodic motive from m. 1 has been turned upside down or inverted. Measure 6 uses an inversion of m. 2.

Measure 7 introduces both a new high point and a small variation in the rhythm.

As in the earlier answers, the melody ends on the Tonic note, this time approached by step from above ($\hat{2}$ to $\hat{1}$).

Once you have practiced writing several answering phrases that are closely based on the given phrases, you may wish to experiment with some freer versions. Study the remaining answers. How is each related to the given phrase?

2   14.   MELODIES IN MINOR KEYS

Remember that the raised leading note is needed in the V triad in both the perfect and imperfect cadences in minor keys.

If the raised leading note is in the melody, be careful in approaching it. Avoid the melodic intervals of the augmented 2nd and the augmented 4th. The augmented 2nd occurs when the unaltered submediant note steps up to the raised leading note. The augmented 4th occurs when the subdominant note leaps up to the raised leading note.

Avoid:

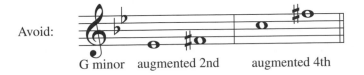

G minor   augmented 2nd   augmented 4th

Example 2

key: _____   _____

Four possible answers are shown on the following pages.

answer 2(a)

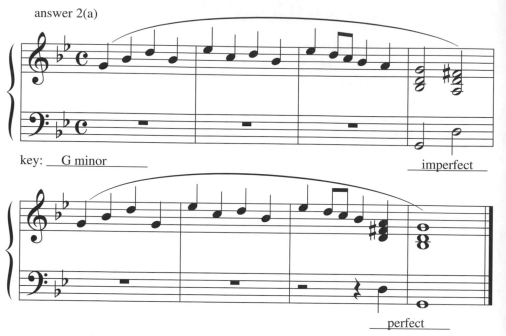

key: ___G minor___   imperfect

___perfect___

Answer 2(a), like answer 1(a), repeats most of the given phrase.

Notice the stepwise approach to the tonic note at the end of the melody, harmonized with a perfect cadence.

answer 2(b)

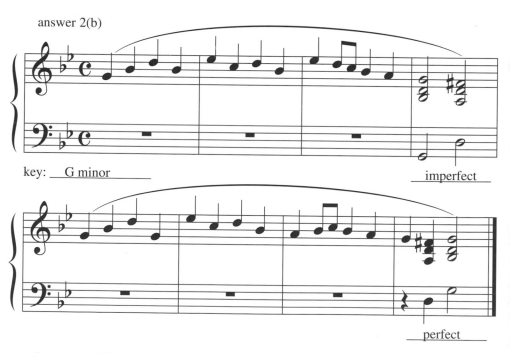

key: ___G minor___   ___imperfect___

___perfect___

In answer 2(b), the melody keeps moving until beat 3 of the final measure.

While melodies typically end on beat 1 of the final measure, not all melodies do so. In $\frac{4}{4}$ meter, ending on beat 3 can be effective. In $\frac{6}{8}$, ending on beat 2 (pulse 4) is quite common.

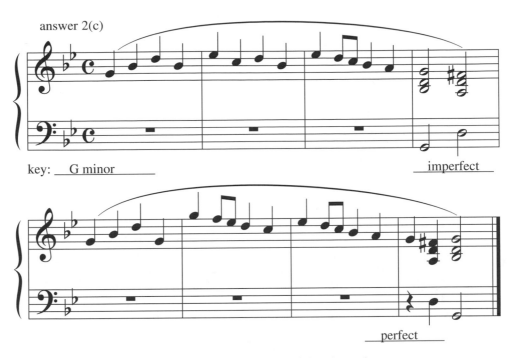

answer 2(c)

key: __G minor__

__imperfect__

__perfect__

Answer 2(c) repeats only the first three notes of the given phrase.

The melodic line includes a new high point.

Note the use of the descending melodic minor scale in m. 6.

The rhythmic motive ♩ ♫ from m. 3 is emphasized in this answer.

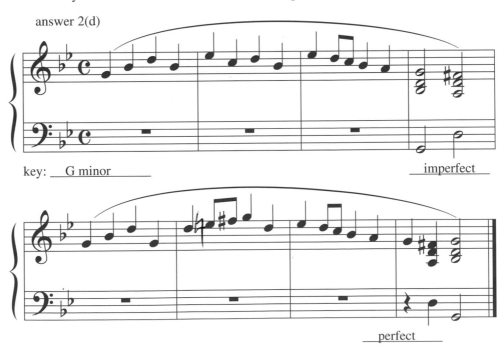

answer 2(d)

key: __G minor__

__imperfect__

__perfect__

Note the use of the ascending melodic minor scale in m. 6. The raised leading note is needed to emphasize the move up to the high tonic; the raised submediant is needed to avoid the augmented 2nd that would occur between E♭ and F♯.

2   EXERCISES

1.   For each of the following:

   • Name the key.
   • Write a cadence at the end of the given phrase and name the cadence.
   • Write an answering phrase for the melody, ending with a perfect cadence.
   • Draw the phrase mark for your answering phrase.

   Suggestion: For each given phrase in the following exercises, write a response that is closely based on phrase 1. Concentrate on making the final cadence as convincing as possible. Then, on manuscript paper, write one or more additional answers to each opening, trying some of the techniques shown in the examples above. Be sure to sing or play each of your melodies.

a)

key: _____   _____

b)

key: _____   _____

c)

key: _____   _____

d)

key: _____   _____

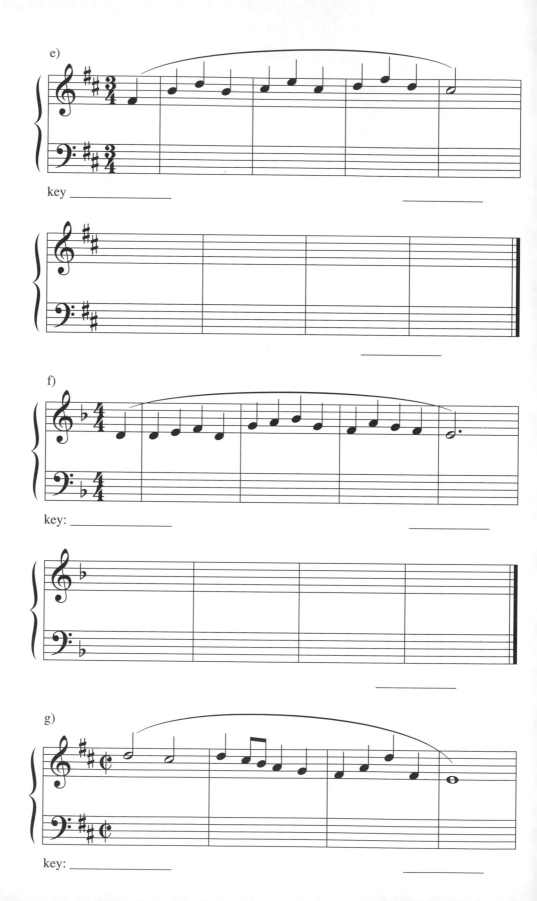

e)

key _____   _____

f)

key: _____   _____

g)

key: _____   _____

h)

key: _____   _____

i)

key: _____   _____

j)

key: _____   _____

k)

key: _____   _____

CHAPTER 7

TIME

SIMPLE TIME

P 1 2   1.   Music is an art that exists in the dimension of TIME. Time is measured by recurring PULSES or BEATS, some stronger than others. A beat that is stronger than another is called an accented beat, or more simply, an ACCENT.

P 1 2   2.   Beats group themselves into two, three, or four at a time. (All beats and subdivisions of beats are in twos or threes, or multiples of twos or threes.) Each group of beats is called a BAR or MEASURE, and the first beat of every measure has the strongest accent. A vertical line called a BAR LINE is placed on the staff immediately before this accent to show its position. A DOUBLE BAR LINE is placed at the end of a piece. A measure can contain notes, rests, or a combination of both.

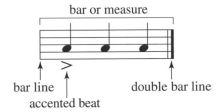

P 1 2   3.   The measuring of music into beats with their recurring accents is called METER or TIME. RHYTHM is a far broader term, that includes meter, melody, harmony, and the whole movement of the music through the grouping of measures into phrases, phrases into sentences, and sentences into a completely integrated piece of music.

P 1 2   4.   Unless a change is indicated, the number of beats in each measure will be the same throughout a piece of music. Therefore, a sign called a TIME SIGNATURE (which has two numbers, one above the other) is placed at the beginning of the music, right after the key signature. Unlike the key signature, it is not repeated at the beginning of each staff, but is just placed at the start, or where a change of time necessitates a new time signature.

P 1 2   5.   In SIMPLE TIME, the upper figure of the time signature tells us how many beats there are in each measure, and the lower figure tells us what kind of a note gets one beat. The upper figure is usually 2, 3, or 4, which are called DUPLE, TRIPLE, or QUADRUPLE respectively. The lower figure can be 1, 2, 4, 8, or 16, to indicate the relative lengths of notes in use in the piece.

180

P 1 2   Thus: 1 represents a whole note

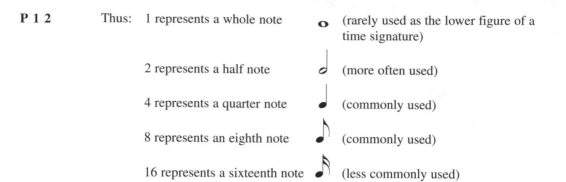

2 represents a half note   (more often used)

4 represents a quarter note   (commonly used)

8 represents an eighth note   (commonly used)

16 represents a sixteenth note   (less commonly used)

P 1 2   6.   In SIMPLE DUPLE TIME, the accent occurs once every two beats.

| 1 | 2 | 1 | 2 ||
strong | weak | strong | weak

The upper number of the time signature will be 2; since the lower number represents a *kind* of note, the possible simple duple time signatures are **2/2** (sometimes called "alla breve" or "cut-time" and indicated by **¢**), **2/4**, **2/8**, and rarely **2/16**.

Simple duple time

2 half notes in a measure   2 quarter notes in a measure   2 eighth notes in a measure

P 1 2   7.   In SIMPLE TRIPLE TIME, the accent occurs once every three beats.

| 1 | 2 | 3 | 1 | 2 | 3 ||
strong | weak | weak | strong | weak | weak

Here, of course, the upper number of the time signature will be 3, and the possible time signatures are **3/2**, **3/4** (waltz time), **3/8**, and rarely **3/16**.

Simple triple time

3 half notes in a measure   3 quarter notes in a measure   3 eighth notes in a measure

P 1 2 8. In SIMPLE QUADRUPLE TIME, the accent occurs once every four beats.

	1	2	3	4	1	2	3	4	
	strong	weak	medium	weak	strong	weak	medium	weak	

It is almost like two measures of duple time combined into one, except that the third beat does not have as strong an accent as the first. The most common of all time signatures is $\frac{4}{4}$ (often indicated by C and called common time); however, $\frac{4}{2}$, $\frac{4}{8}$, and $\frac{4}{16}$ are also possible time signatures in this category.

Simple quadruple time

4 half notes in a measure   4 quarter notes in a measure   4 eighth notes in a measure

P 1 2 9. Study the following examples of rhythms in simple time and note that:

- Not all the rhythms start on an accented beat. In these cases, the time of the incomplete bar at the beginning, called an UPBEAT, is deducted from the time of the last measure. In other words, the time of the last measure + the time of the upbeat = 1 full measure.

- All the notes constituting one beat are grouped together, in order to make the divisions of the measure easy to read.

P 1 2 10. Rests also must be fitted into the measure in such a way as to show the beats as clearly as possible. Do not use rests of greater value than one beat, except at the first half or last half of a measure of quadruple time.

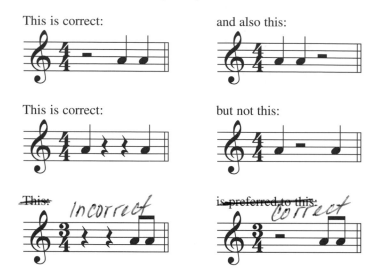

This is correct: and also this:

This is correct: but not this:

This: *Incorrect*   is preferred to this: *Correct*

It is important to remember that each beat must be completed before the next on is begun, and each part of the beat must be completed before starting the next part.

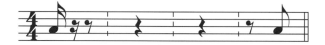

A whole measure's rest in almost any time signature is represented by a whole rest. The exception is $\frac{4}{2}$ time: in $\frac{4}{2}$ time, the breve rest is used, since the whole rest represents only half the measure in this time signature.

P 1 2 11. A TRIPLET is a group of three equal notes that are meant to be played in the time of two notes of the same value.

Examples:

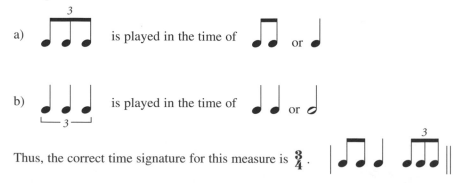

a) is played in the time of   or

b) is played in the time of   or

Thus, the correct time signature for this measure is $\frac{3}{4}$.

P 1 2 12. Play these short melodies by Bach, in order to get the feeling of a recurring accent in each of the three kinds of simple time.

Musette, BWV Anh 126

simple duple

Minuet, BWV Anh 114

simple triple

Bourrée from Partita for Solo Violin, BWV 1002

simple quadruple

P 1 2 **EXERCISES**

1. Write two measures, each using a different rhythm, for each of the following time signatures.

Example:

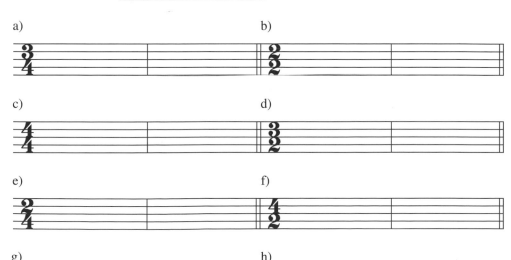

a) $\frac{3}{4}$

b) $\frac{2}{2}$

c) $\frac{4}{4}$

d) $\frac{3}{2}$

e) $\frac{2}{4}$

f) $\frac{4}{2}$

g) $\frac{3}{8}$

h) $\frac{4}{8}$

184

2. Add bar lines to each of the following according to the given time signature.

a)

b)

c)

d)

e)

f)

g)

h)

3. Add the correct time signature to each of the following rhythms.

a)

b)

c)

d)

e)

f)

g)

h)

i)

j)

4. Add bar lines to each of the following according to the given time signature.

a)

b)

c)

d)

e)

f)

g)

h)

5. Complete the following measures with rests in the places indicated by the brackets.

a)

188

6.	Add stems to the following and group them correctly to make one complete measure in each of the following time signatures.

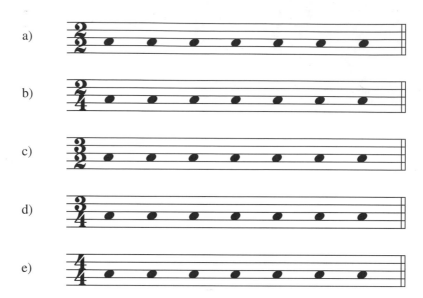

a)

b)

c)

d)

e)

7.	Add the correct time signature to each of the following measures.

a)

b)

c)

d)

e)

COMPOUND TIME

1 2 13. There are two basic categories of time signatures—SIMPLE and COMPOUND. COMPOUND TIME is divided into the same three groups as simple time, called COMPOUND DUPLE (meaning two), COMPOUND TRIPLE (meaning three), and COMPOUND QUADRUPLE (meaning four).

SPECIAL NOTE: While the term PULSE is normally used to refer to a beat, for the purpose of explaining compound time clearly, the word "pulse" here will refer to a DIVISION of a beat, and not to the beat itself. (For example, in $\frac{6}{8}$ time, each eighth note is a pulse.)

1 2 14. The difference between simple and compound time is that whereas in simple time each beat can be represented by one single undotted note, in compound time each beat is divisible into three parts, and therefore is equal to a dotted note. No number exists that can be used as the lower figure of a time signature to represent a dotted note, so of necessity the upper figure of the time signature in compound time tells the number of PULSES in each measure rather than the number of beats, and the lower figure tells the time value of each pulse. You will see that if the upper number is divided by three, it will give the number of beats for each measure.

1 2   15.   COMPOUND DUPLE TIME has two beats in a measure, with three pulses in each beat. Therefore, the upper figure of the time signature is 6 and the lower figure will be the one that represents one pulse: $\frac{6}{4}$, $\frac{6}{8}$, or $\frac{6}{16}$.

Example: $\frac{6}{8}$ indicates 6 eighth-note pulses in a measure, divided into two groups three, each group constituting one beat equal to a dotted quarter note.

compound duple time

2 dotted half notes   2 dotted quarter notes   2 dotted eighth notes
in a measure   in a measure   in a measure

1 2   16.   COMPOUND TRIPLE TIME, like simple triple time, has three beats in a measure. Since each beat contains three pulses, the top figure is 9. The possible time signatures are $\frac{9}{4}$, $\frac{9}{8}$, and $\frac{9}{16}$.

compound triple time

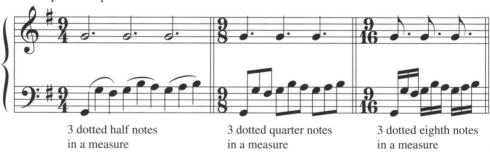

3 dotted half notes   3 dotted quarter notes   3 dotted eighth notes
in a measure   in a measure   in a measure

1 2   17.   Since COMPOUND QUADRUPLE TIME has four beats in a measure, the upper figure must be 12. The possible time signatures in compound quadruple time are $\frac{12}{4}$, $\frac{12}{8}$, and $\frac{12}{16}$.

compound quadruple time

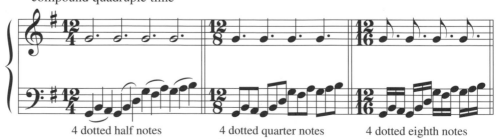

4 dotted half notes   4 dotted quarter notes   4 dotted eighth notes
in a measure   in a measure   in a measure

1 2   18.   The following chart compares simple and compound time signatures.

	SIMPLE TIME	COMPOUND TIME
DUPLE (2 beats)	$\frac{2}{2}$ 𝅗𝅥 𝅗𝅥 $\frac{2}{4}$ ♩ ♩ $\frac{2}{8}$ ♪ ♪	$\frac{6}{4}$ 𝅗𝅥. 𝅗𝅥. $\frac{6}{8}$ ♩. ♩. $\frac{6}{16}$ ♪. ♪.
TRIPLE (3 beats)	$\frac{3}{2}$ 𝅗𝅥 𝅗𝅥 𝅗𝅥 $\frac{3}{4}$ ♩ ♩ ♩ $\frac{3}{8}$ ♪ ♪ ♪	$\frac{9}{4}$ 𝅗𝅥. 𝅗𝅥. 𝅗𝅥. $\frac{9}{8}$ ♩. ♩. ♩. $\frac{9}{16}$ ♪. ♪. ♪.
QUADRUPLE (4 beats)	$\frac{4}{2}$ 𝅗𝅥 𝅗𝅥 𝅗𝅥 𝅗𝅥 $\frac{4}{4}$ ♩ ♩ ♩ ♩ $\frac{4}{8}$ ♪ ♪ ♪ ♪	$\frac{12}{4}$ 𝅗𝅥. 𝅗𝅥. 𝅗𝅥. 𝅗𝅥. $\frac{12}{8}$ ♩. ♩. ♩. ♩. $\frac{12}{16}$ ♪. ♪. ♪. ♪.

1 2   19.   As in simple time, notes and rests in compound time are grouped so as to make the divisions of the beats as clear as possible. All the notes belonging to one beat are grouped together.

It is important to note that in compound time, the first and second pulses of each beat should be represented by one rest, but the second and third pulses are always given separate rests. In compound time, a dotted rest is used to indicate one full beat. As in simple time, a complete measure of silence is indicated by a whole rest.

These are both correct:

These are both incorrect:

In compound quadruple time, as in simple quadruple time, the first half and the last half of the measure must be represented by one dotted rest.

1 2　20.　Play the following three melodies, also by Bach, so that you can feel the accents and pulses in each of the three kinds of compound time.

Siciliano from Sonata for Flute and Keyboard, BWV 1031

compound duple

Little Prelude, BWV 942

compound triple

Sinfonia no. 2, BWV 788

compound quadruple

SYNCOPATION AND IRREGULAR GROUPS

1 2　21.　SYNCOPATION is a disturbing of the natural accent by putting an emphasis on what is normally a weak part of the measure. In other words, syncopation shifts the accent temporarily from a strong to a weak beat.

1 2　22.　Besides the triplet (see paragraph 11, p. 182), there are many other irregular subdivisions of beats used by composers that must be fitted into the regular beats of the measure. The number of these subdivisions is shown at the beam or at the notehead.

They are to be played in the same time as the normal group of notes of the same kind, according to the time signature.

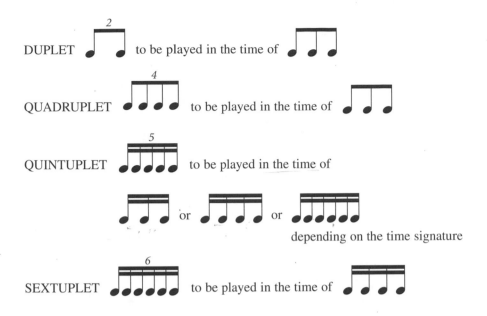

This is not as complicated as it looks. The best way to calculate these changes of note values is to look at the measure as a whole, and then fit the group into the time required to fill up the irregular part.

1 2 EXERCISES

1. Complete the following measures with rests in the places indicated by the brackets.

2. Add the correct time signature to each of the following measures.

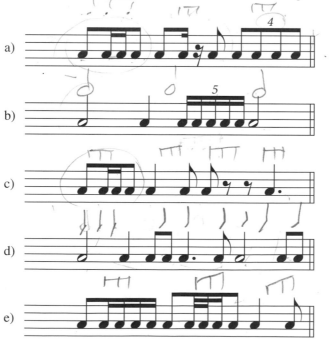

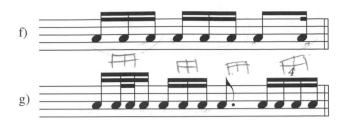

f)

g)

3.   Add bar lines to each of the following according to the given time signatures.

a)

b)

c)

d)

e)

f)

g)

4. Add stems to the following, and group them correctly to make *one* complete measure in each of the following time signatures.

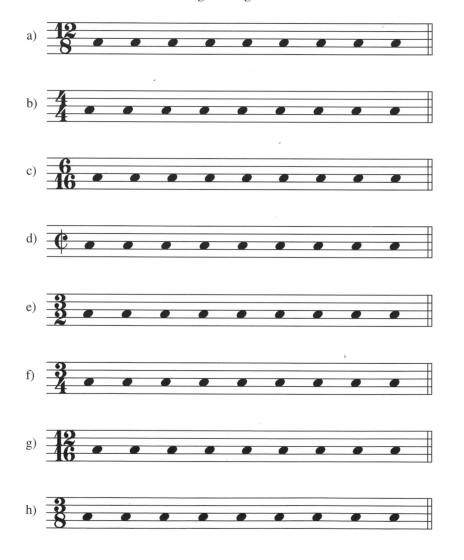

5. Regroup the following in $\frac{6}{8}$ time.

6. Regroup the following in $\frac{3}{4}$ time.

7. a) What is the difference between $\frac{6}{8}$ time and $\frac{3}{4}$ time?

   b) Write one measure of each, grouping the notes correctly.

   a) The difference is: _____

   _____

   b)

8. Write three measures, each using a different rhythm, in each of the following time signatures. You may use dotted notes but not rests.

a)

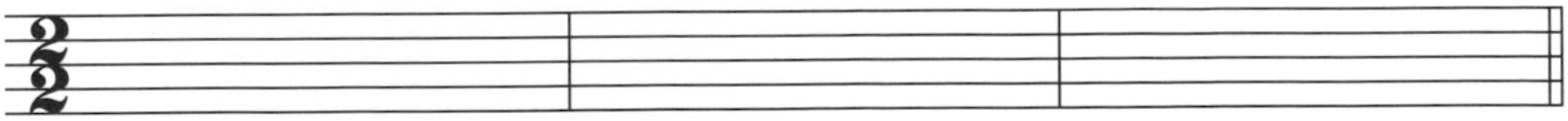

b)

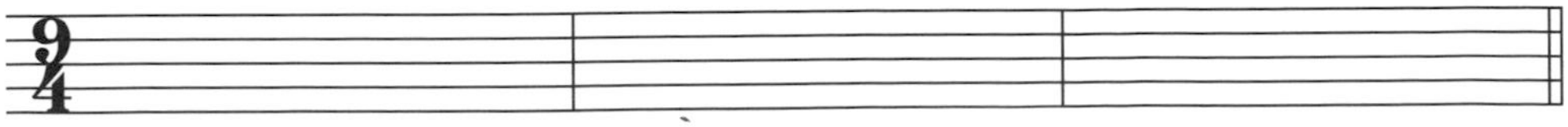

c)

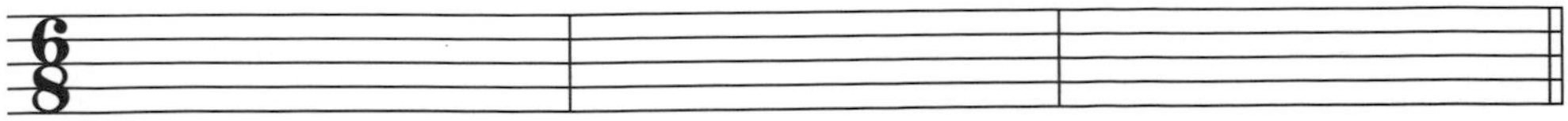

198

d)

e)

f)

g)

h)

i)

9. Complete the following measures with rests.

a)

b)

c)

d)

e)

10. Complete the following measures with rests.

MIXED METERS

2 23. In simple time, the beats are plain undotted notes. For example, in $\frac{2}{4}$ time, we count two quarter notes.

In compound time, the pulses are organized in groups of three, resulting in beats that are dotted notes. For example, in $\frac{6}{8}$ meter, we count two dotted quarter notes.

In mixed meters, both plain and dotted beats occur in each measure. As in compound time, the lower number of the time signature represents the kind of note that gets the pulse. The upper number tells us the number of pulses in each measure.

Examples **5** ← There are 5 pulses per measure.
8 ← The eighth note is the pulse.

7 ← There are 7 pulses per measure.
4 ← The quarter note is the pulse.

Mixed meters differ from compound time in that there is more than one way of grouping pulses into beats for each hybrid time signature.

2 24. HYBRID DUPLE TIME

Hybrid duple time has two beats to a measure. The upper number of the time signature is 5. One of the beats has 3 pulses and the other has 2. Either the dotted or the undotted beat can come first.

Example

A well-known example of $\frac{5}{4}$ time is from Tchaikovsky's Symphony No. 6 ("Pathétique"), op. 74.

2 25. HYBRID TRIPLE TIME

Hybrid triple time has three beats to a measure. The upper number of the time signature is 7. One of the beats has 3 pulses and the other two beats each have 2 pulses.

Example

Alternately, $\frac{7}{4}$ may be seen as 3 + 4 or 4 + 3.

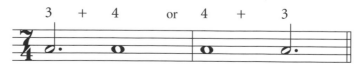

2   26.   **HYBRID QUADRUPLE TIME**

Hybrid quadruple time is less common than hybrid duple or triple time. It has four beats to a measure. The upper number of the time signature may vary; it usually 10 or 11. There are several different groupings possible.

Examples

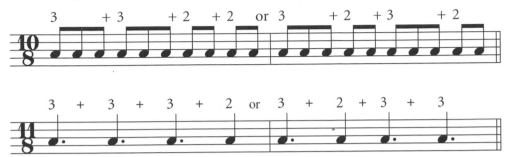

A piece of music written in a mixed meter may maintain the same grouping throughout, or the grouping may change from measure to measure. For example, a piece in hybrid duple meter may be 3 + 2 throughout, or it may contain some measures of 3 + 2 and others of 2 + 3.

2   27.   **ADDING RESTS**

When you are asked to add rests to a given incomplete measure of a mixed meter, the first step is to decide on the grouping. In some cases, the given notes will make the grouping obvious.

In m. 1, three quarter notes have been grouped together for the first beat, so the remaining two quarter notes must be grouped for beat 2.

In m. 2, the last two quarter notes have been grouped to form the second beat, so we need to add a group of three.

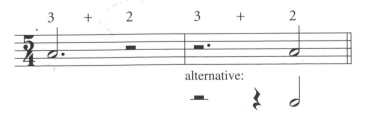

In other cases, the given notes will not make clear the group of the pulses into beats.

Example: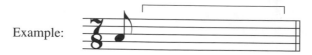

When this occurs, *you* must decide on the grouping. There will be more than one correct answer. You must choose some grouping, however, and not simply indicate seven separate beats.

These are all correct:

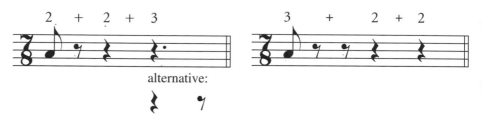

If $\frac{7}{8}$ is viewed as $\frac{3}{8} + \frac{4}{8}$, then:

would also be acceptable.

This is incorrect:

Just as in simple and compound time, a whole rest (or, in certain time signatures, a breve rest) is used to indicate an entire measure of silence.

Examples

2   EXERCISES

1.   Complete the following measures with notes showing the two different ways of grouping duple meters.

Example:

a)

b)

c)

2.   Complete the following measures with notes showing the five different ways of grouping hybrid triple meters.

Example:

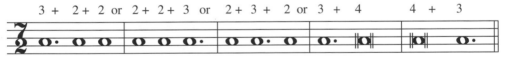

a)

b)

c)

3. Add a time signature to each of the following, and indicate the grouping of the pulses into beats.

Example:

4.   Complete the following measures with rests in the places indicated by the brackets.

CHAPTER 8

NAMING THE KEY, TRANSPOSITION, AND DETECTING ERRORS

FINDING THE KEY OF A GIVEN MELODY

P 1 2   1.   If the melody is written USING A KEY SIGNATURE, the solution is not difficult. Automatically, you have a choice of only two keys—the major and its relative minor.

This melody contains no accidentals, only diatonic notes in the scale of B♭ major.

This one contains an F♯, the raised leading note of G minor.

Occasionally, you will encounter a melody which is in a minor key but does not contain the raised leading note.

A melody in a minor key may use any or all of the three forms of the minor scale: harmonic, melodic, or natural. Depending on which form of the scale is used, the leading note may or may not be raised; the submediant note also may or may not be raised.

Many melodies use only the first five or six notes of the scale. In these melodies, the leading note does not appear. You may also encounter melodies that contain accidentals other than the raised leading note of a minor key. It is important to consider several aspects of the melody before you decide on the name of its key.

1. The *key signature*: Consider both the major key and the minor key represented by a given key signature.

2. *Accidentals*: Could an accidental be the raised leading note of the minor key? Could it be the raised submediant note of the melodic minor scale? Or does it affect some other scale degree, in major or minor (i.e., chromaticism)?

3. Consider the *final note*. Most melodies end on the tonic note. However, not all melodies do so. Also, you may be given an excerpt only, and so you will not see the end of the melody.

4. Consider the *opening notes*. Often melodies begin on the tonic or dominant notes. If a melody begins with an upbeat, looking at the first downbeat is also helpful. Opening notes are, however, a much less reliable guide to key than the other factors since, in fact, a melody may begin on any scale degree.

5. Look for places in which the melody skips along the notes of a *triad*. The most common triads are I, IV, and V, although, of course, any triad may occur.

It is important to remember that the above points are guidelines only. No single one of them is a completely reliable guide to naming the key of a melody, and all applicable points should be considered.

Take time and be careful when naming the key of a given melody. Often you will be asked to continue with other steps, such as transposing the melody, writing another phrase, or adding cadences to the melody. Naming the key correctly is vital for the success of the other steps.

Study the following examples:

Example 1

1. The key signature of three flats means that the key could be either E♭ major or C minor.
2. There are no accidentals. There is no B♮ (raised leading note of C minor), but note that there are no B♭'s cither.
3. The melody ends on C.
4. It begins on C. } Is this more likely $\hat{6}$ of E♭ major or $\hat{1}$ or C minor?
5. The melody begins by outlining a C minor triad, C–E♭–G. (VI of E♭ major or I of C minor?)

Answer: The key is C minor.

Example 2

1. The key signature of one sharp means that the key could be either G major or E minor.
2. There are no accidentals. D♮, not D♯, occurs in m. 1; there are no other D's, ♮ or ♯.
3. The melody ends on E.
4. It begins on B, with E on the downbeat.
5. There are no obvious outlines of triads, so point 5 will not help in this case.

Answer: The key is E minor. Note that D♮ occurs in a descending scale passage.

1 2   Example 3

1. The key signature of two sharps means that the key could be either D major or B minor.

2. There is a G♯ near the beginning. Could G♯ be the raised submediant note of the B melodic minor scale? Note that there are also two G♮'s, and all of the A's are natural.

3. The melody ends on E. Is this the supertonic of D major or the subdominant of B minor? In either case, the melody is incomplete.

4. The melody starts on A. The first downbeat is D. The leap A to D recurs in m. 1.

Answer: The key is D major. The G♯ is chromatic decoration, not part of the scale of the melody.

P 1 2   EXERCISES

1.   Name the key of each of the following melodies.

a)

key:_____

b)

key:_____

c)

key:_____

209

d)

key:_____

e)

key:_____

f)

key:_____

g)

key:_____

h)

key:_____

210

i)

key:_____

1 2 MORE EXERCISES

1.   Name the key of each of the following melodies.

a)

key:_____

b)

key:_____

c)

key:_____

1 2 2. IF NO KEY SIGNATURE is used, just accidentals, determining the key is more difficult.

If the accidentals are all *sharps,* write down the order in which sharps appear in a key signature, and then check them off as you find them in the melody.

Example 1

F̌ Č G D A E B

Since this melody has only the first two sharps, the key could be D major or B minor. There are several A naturals; the melody begins on A and ends on D. The key is D major.

Example 2

F̌ Č Ǧ D A E B

The only sharps appearing in the accepted order are F♯ and C♯. Therefore, A♯ must be an accidental. Try it as the raised leading note of a minor key, and you will find the key to be B minor, whose key signature is two sharps.

Example 3

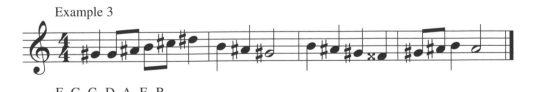

F̌ Č Ǧ Ď Ǎ E B

The first five sharps appear in order in this melody, but the F♯ is raised to an F× Therefore, since it must be the raised leading note, you arrive at the key of G♯ minor, which has the key signature of five sharps.

Summary: If all the sharps in the melody can be arranged in a proper order to form a key signature, the key is likely the major one containing that number of sharps, but if one sharp does *not* logically fit into the right order, then see if it is the raised leading note of the relative minor key.

1 2 3. If the accidentals are all *flats*, write down the order that flats appear in a key signature, and check them off just as you did with the sharps.

Example 1

B E A D G C F

A key signature of three flats accounts for every accidental in this melody, so the key may be E♭ major or C minor. The melody outlines an E♭ major triad in mm. 1–2, and it ends on E♭. The key is E♭ major.

Example 2

B E A D G C F

Here, in order to have E♭ and A♭ in a key signature, you must also have a B♭ to go before them. So try three flats, with the B raised: you arrive at the key of C minor.

Summary: If all the flats can be arranged in the proper order for a flat key signature, the key is likely major, but if one of the flats that should be in the key signature is a natural, then that one will probably be the raised leading note of the relative minor key.

1 2 4. If the accidentals are sharps and flats *mixed*, try using a flat key signature with the sharpened note as the raised leading note.

A key signature of one flat indicates F major or D minor. The raised leading note of D minor is C sharp. The key is D minor.

It now becomes apparent that when you are trying to find the key of a given melody, the note that gives you the best clue is the misfit—the extra sharp, the double sharp, the missing flat, or the sharp among the flats, which will be the leading note of your minor key.

1 2   5.   Naturally, many melodies do not contain every degree of the scale.

When you check off the sharps here, you get F̌ C Ǧ Ď A E B—a rather odd assortment of sharps until you realize that there is no C of any kind in the melody. In order to account for the other sharps, you can assume that if there were a C, it would be a C sharp, and the key, therefore, would be E major.

TRANSPOSITION

P 1 2   6.   TRANSPOSITION generally means a change of pitch. It is often used in songs, to accommodate the range of a singer's voice. The word can also mean a change of clef without a change of pitch.

P 1 2   7.   **TRANSPOSITION UP AN OCTAVE**

This means that the melody must be rewritten so that each note will sound an octave higher than in the original. This may or may not involve a change of clef.

Method: Put the required clef, key signature, and time signature on the staff, then carefully calculate where the first note will have to go on the new staff to sound an octave higher. It helps to remember that middle C is the link between the staves.

When this note 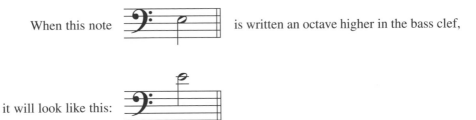 is written an octave higher in the bass clef,

it will look like this:

but the original note written an octave higher in the treble clef will be:

After you have decided where the first note goes, just follow the melody line, going up or down the required intervals each time, and being careful to face the stems the right way.

Here is a given melody.

Here it is transposed up an octave in the bass clef.

Here it is transposed up an octave from the original, but in the treble clef.

8.   TRANSPOSITION DOWN AN OCTAVE involves exactly the same procedure as the above.

P 1 2   EXERCISES

1.   Name the key of the following melody. Transpose it down an octave in the treble clef.

key:_____

2.   Name the key of the following melody. Transpose it up an octave in the bass clef.

key:_____

3.   Name the key of the following melody. Transpose it up an octave into the treble clef.

key:_____

4.   Name the key of the following melody. Transpose it down an octave into the bass clef.

key:_____

5.   Name the key of the following melody. Transpose it down an octave in the treble clef.

key:_____

6.   Name the key of the following melody. Transpose it down an octave into the bass clef.

key:_____

7.   Name the key of the following melody. Transpose it up an octave into the treble clef.

key:_____

8.   Name the key of the following melody. Transpose it down an octave into the bass clef.

key:_____

9.   Name the key of the following melody. Transpose it down an octave into the bass clef.

key:_____

10.   Name the key of the following melody. Transpose it down an octave into the bass clef.

key:_____

11.   Name the key of the following melody. Transpose it up an octave into the treble clef.

key:_____

12.   Name the key of the following melody. Transpose it down an octave in the bass clef.

key:_____

218

13.   Name the key of the following melody. Transpose it up an octave into the treble clef.

key:_____

14.   Name the key of the following melody. Transpose it down an octave in the treble clef.

key:_____

15.   Name the key of the following melody. Transpose it down an octave into the bass clef.

key:_____

1 2   MORE EXERCISES

1.   Name the key of the following melody. Rewrite it at the same pitch using the correct key signature and omitting any unnecessary accidentals.

key:_____

2.   Name the key of the following melody. Transpose it down an octave into the bass clef.

key:_____

3.   Name the key of the following melody. Transpose it down an octave into the bass clef.

key:_____

_____

4.   Name the key of the following melody. Rewrite it at the same pitch in the treble clef, using the correct key signature and omitting any unnecessary accidentals.

key:_____

_____

_____

5.   Name the key of the following melody. Transpose it down an octave into the bass clef, using the correct key signature and omitting any unnecessary accidentals.

key:_____

_____

6. Name the key of the following melody. Transpose it up an octave in the bass clef, using the correct key signature and omitting any unnecessary accidentals.

key:_____

7. Name the key of the following melody. Transpose it down an octave into the bass clef, using the correct key signature and omitting any unnecessary accidentals.

key:_____

2 STILL MORE EXERCISES

1. Name the key of the following melody. Rewrite it at the same pitch in the alto clef, using the correct key signature and omitting any unnecessary accidentals.

key:_____

2. Name the key of the following melody. Transpose it up an octave into the treble clef.

key:_____

3.   Name the key of the following melody. Rewrite it at the same pitch in the alto clef, using the correct key signature and omitting any unnecessary accidentals.

key:_____

4.   Name the key of the following melody. Rewrite it an octave lower in the alto clef, using the correct key signature and omitting any unnecessary accidentals.

key:_____

TRANSPOSITION INVOLVING A CHANGE OF KEY OR CLEF

1 2 Transposition can be made from one major key to any other major key, and from one minor key to any other minor key.

1 2 9. **HERE ARE THE STEPS FOR TRANSPOSITION FROM ONE MAJOR KEY TO ANOTHER**

1. Before you can attempt transposition of a melody, you must identify the original key, as discussed earlier in this chapter.

2. The name of the new key must also be found. Frequently, instead of saying "Transpose this melody into the key of B♭ major," the question will be worded "Transpose this melody up a major 3rd." In this case, you must be sure that the tonic of the new key is a major 3rd above the tonic of the old key.

3. Having found the new key, write its key signature.

4. Remembering what size interval exists between old 1̂ and new 1̂, move each note up (or down) the right distance, *by letter name only*. The relative positions of the notes do not change, and the new key signature automatically takes care of the quality of the interval.

5. After the notes are written on their proper lines and spaces, then add an accidental in the new version to correspond with each accidental in the original. You will have to select the one that has the same *effect,* realizing that it will not necessarily be the same *kind* of accidental because of the change of key signature.

Question: Transpose the following melody downward into D major.

Answer: The key of the given passage is E♭ major. From E♭ to D is down a 2nd. So, having put the key signature of two sharps, move each note down a 2nd.

Then insert the two accidentals to correspond with those in the original. The first must raise the note a semitone, the second must lower it a semitone.

Question: Transpose the original melody up a major 3rd.

Answer: The major 3rd above E♭ is G, so the new key is G major. Put in the key signature of G major, and then move each note up a 3rd. Then insert the accidentals to raise the first one and lower the second, as before.

2 10. TRANSPOSITION FROM MINOR TO MINOR should create no new problems. If you are not sure whether the given melody is major or minor, remember if the new key asked for is stated as being minor ("transpose this into F minor"), then the original must of course be minor.

Question: Transpose this melody up a minor 2nd.

Answer: Since this melody is in E minor, a minor 2nd up would be F minor, which has a key signature of four flats.

2 11. A CHANGE OF CLEF can always go along with a change of key, but with careful thought this should not create too much difficulty. Always use middle C as your connecting link between the clefs, and if at first you find it too complicated to change both key and clef at once, take time first to transpose the melody into the correct key and then re-write it in the proper clef.

Question: Transpose the following into C major, using the alto clef.

You may find it better to do this:

before you do this:

2 12. IF THE TRANSPOSITION IS IN FOUR PARTS, it is wise to take each part separately, and if the question also asks for a change from short to open score, you are strongly advised to attempt only one step at a time. Transpose first and then change to open score. (See Chapter 9.)

2 . 13.   Altering a melody from major key to minor key and vice versa, is *not* a transposition, but a change of mode. Here is an example:

In D major

In D minor

Obviously, these do not sound the same, as the third and the sixth degrees of the minor key are lower than those of the major.

1 2   EXERCISES

1.   Transpose the following melody into A major.

key:_____

2.   Transpose the following melody a) into F major b) up a major 3rd. Name the new key.

key:_____

a)

b)

key:_____

3.   Transpose the following melody a) into G major b) up a perfect 4th. Name the
      new key.

key:_____

a)

b)

key:_____

4.   Transpose the following melody a) up a major 2nd and name the new key
      b) into A major.

key:_____

a)

key:_____

b)

5. Transpose the following melody a) up a perfect 4th b) up a major 2nd. In each case, name the new key.

key:_____

a)

key:_____

b)

key:_____

6. Transpose the following melody a) up a major 3rd and name the new key
b) into G major.

key:_____

a)

key:_____

b)

7. Transpose the following melody a) into B♭ major b) into F major.

key:_____

a)

b)

8. In what key is the following melody written? Transpose it into D major, using the correct key signature.

key:_____

9.   Transpose the following melody a) into A major b) up a major 3rd. Name the new key.

key:_____

a)

_____

b)

_____

key:_____

10. Transpose the following melody a) into D♭ major b) up a minor 3rd. Name the new key.

key:_____

a)

_____

b)

_____

key:_____

2 MORE EXERCISES

1.   Transpose the following melody down a major 2nd. Name the new key.

key:_____

key:_____

2.   Transpose the following melody up a major 2nd. Name the new key.

key:_____

key:_____

3.   Transpose the following melody down a major 2nd. Name the new key.

key:_____

key:_____

4. Transpose the following melody down a major 2nd. Name the new key.

key:_____

key:_____

5. Transpose the following melody up a minor 3rd into the alto clef. Name the new key.

key:_____

key:_____

6. In what key is the following melody written? Transpose it into G minor, using the correct key signature and omitting any unnecessary accidentals.

key:_____

7.   In what key is the following melody written? Transpose it down a major 3rd, using the correct key signature and omitting any unnecessary accidentals. Name the new key.

key:_____

key:_____

8.   In what key is the following melody written? Transpose it a) into G minor b) into B♭ minor, using the correct key signature and omitting any unnecessary accidentals.

key:_____

a)

b)

9. In what key is the following melody written? Transpose it into E minor, using the correct key signature and omitting any unnecessary accidentals.

key:_____

10. Transpose the following melody a) into B minor b) up a major 3rd. Name the new key.

key:_____

a)

b)

key:_____

11. In what key is the following melody written? Transpose it a) down a minor 3rd
b) up a minor 2nd, using the correct key signature and omitting any unnecessary
accidentals. In each case, name the new key.

key:_____

a)

key:_____

b)

key:_____

12. Transpose the following melody a) into E♭ major b) into B♭ major.

key: _D+_____

a)

b)

INTRODUCTION TO TRANSPOSING INSTRUMENTS

2 14. TRANSPOSING INSTRUMENTS produce a pitch different from that of the notated pitch.

The piano is *not* a transposing instrument. If a pianist reads a note, for example, middle C, she or he plays middle C and hears middle C as a result. Therefore, we say that the piano is a C instrument.

In contrast to this, the clarinet, for example, *is* a transposing instrument. There are many different sizes of clarinets, but the most common one is the B♭ clarinet. On this instrument, if a player reads a C, and plays a C, the resulting pitch is actually a B♭, a major 2nd lower than the written pitch. The actual sounding pitch (in this case, the B♭) is called the CONCERT PITCH.

Transposing instruments are named after the concert pitch that sounds when they play a written C. The four instruments we will study here are:

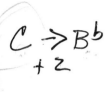

- the clarinet in B♭
- the trumpet in B♭
- the French horn in F

These three instruments come in different sizes (with different transpositions) so the key is stated.

- the English horn (in F)

The English horn (actually a large oboe rather than a horn) only comes in F, so the key may not be stated.

The concert pitch of a transposing instrument may be higher or lower than the written pitch. The four instruments listed above all sound *lower* than the written pitch.

The clarinet in B♭ and the trumpet in B♭ both sound a major 2nd lower than written:

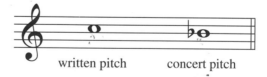

written pitch   concert pitch

The French horn in F and the English horn both sound a perfect 5th lower than written:

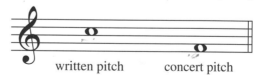

written pitch   concert pitch

Do not confuse the key of an instrument with the key of the music it plays. The designation "in B♭" or "in F" tells you nothing about the key in which a melody is written. If the melody is written in C (major or minor), then at concert pitch it will be in B♭ (major or minor) or in F (major or minor), depending on the instrument that plays it. If the melody is written in any other key than C, then at concert pitch it will *not* be in the keys of B♭ or F. You will have to figure out the new key.

Example: The following passage is for clarinet in B♭. Name the key in which it is written. Transpose it to concert pitch, using the appropriate new key signature. Name the new key.

Clarinet in B♭

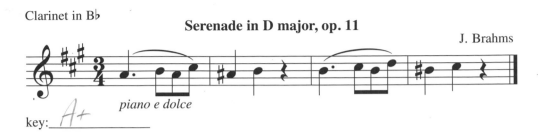

Serenade in D major, op. 11

J. Brahms

piano e dolce

key: A+ _____

Steps:

1. Name the original key. In this case, it is A major.

2. Find the new key, based on what you know about the interval of transposition for the specified instrument.

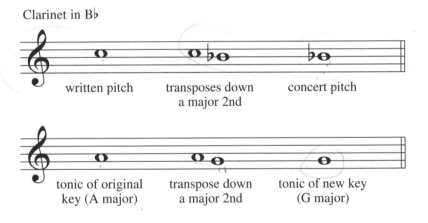

Clarinet in B♭

written pitch   transposes down   concert pitch
                 a major 2nd

tonic of original   transpose down   tonic of new key
key (A major)   a major 2nd   (G major)

3. Name the new key. In this case, it is G major.

4. Write the melody at concert pitch. In addition to transposing the key signature and all pitches correctly, remember to copy all markings form the original into your answer. This includes dynamics, slurs, the composer's name, and anything else that might appear.

Clarinet in B♭

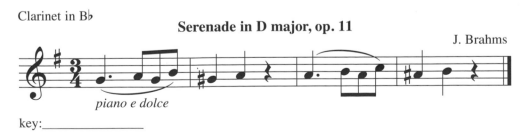

Serenade in D major, op. 11

J. Brahms

piano e dolce

key:_____

2 EXERCISES

1. For each of the following excerpts, name the key in which it is written. Transpose it to concert pitch, using the appropriate new key signature. Name the new key.

a) Trumpet in B♭

The Sleeping Beauty, op. 66, Act I, Valse (No. 6)

Allegro

P.I. Tchaikovsky

ff

key:_____

key:_____

b) French horn in F

Symphony No. 8, op. 93, 3rd movement

Tempo di Menuetto

L. van Beethoven

dolce   *cresc.*

key:_____

key:_____

c) English horn F♯

Harold in Italy ("Serenade"), op. 16, 3rd movement

Allegretto

H. Berlioz

key:_____

key:_____

d) Clarinet in B♭

Symphony No. 3, op. 90, 2nd movement

Andante

J. Brahms

key:_____

key:_____

240

e) English horn

Trio, op. 87

Presto

L. van Beethoven

key:_____

key:_____

f) Clarinet in B♭

Carmen, Acts I–II "Entr'acte"

G. Bizet

Allegretto moderato

key:_____

key:_____

g)   English horn

Overture–Fantaisie, Romeo et Juliette

Allegro giusto

P.I. Tchaikovsky

mf *espr.*

key:_____

key:_____

h)   Clarinet in B♭

A Midsummer Night's Dream, op. 61, "Scherzo"

Allegro vivace

F. Mendelssohn

pp

key:_____

key:_____

DETECTING ERRORS IN A GIVEN PASSAGE OF MUSIC

1 2 15. You may be given a passage of music that purposely contains mistakes. Your job is to find the mistakes, correct them, and rewrite the passage properly. Here are some questions to ask yourself.

1. Is the clef in its correct position on the staff?

2. Do the sharps or flats in the key signature occur in the correct order, and in their proper places?

3. Is the time signature right side up, and *after* the key signature?

4. Are there any bar lines omitted, or any extra ones put in?

5. Are there any double bar lines in the middle of the melody which should be replaced by a single bar line?

6. Is there a double bar line at the end?

7. Are the stems on all the notes facing in the right direction?

8. Are the notes and rests grouped correctly so that they conform to the rules that apply to the given time signature?

9. Are there any tied notes which could be correctly replaced by a single note of equal time-value?

10. Does the piece start with an incomplete measure? If it does, does the last measure contain the fraction of time necessary to complete it?

11. Are any slurs, ties, or other markings drawn incorrectly?

12. Are any musical terms spelled incorrectly?

2 13. Are there any accidentals (or enharmonic changes) that do not logically fit into the key?

1 2 EXERCISES

1. Rewrite the following passages of music, correcting the mistakes.

a)

b)

2   MORE EXERCISES

1.   Rewrite the following passages of music, correcting the mistakes.

a)

b)

c)

d)

Poca agitato

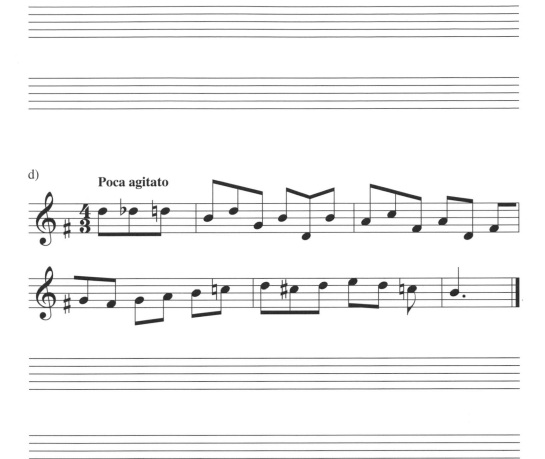

e)

Vivice

CHAPTER 9

SCORE TYPES

2 **1.** A SCORE is a copy of music in which the separate parts are divided, and each part is written (in its appropriate clef) on a separate staff, one underneath the other, so that the whole may be read at a glance.

The title of the work appears centered and the composer's name appears on the right side at the top of the score.

PIANOFORTE score has only two staves, which are connected at the beginning by a system line preceded by a brace. The bar lines go through and connect both staves.

Waltz, op. 39, no. 15

J. Brahms

ORGAN music is normally written on three staves, the lowest one being for the pedal notes that are played with the feet.

Bourrée from **Water Music**

G.F. Handel

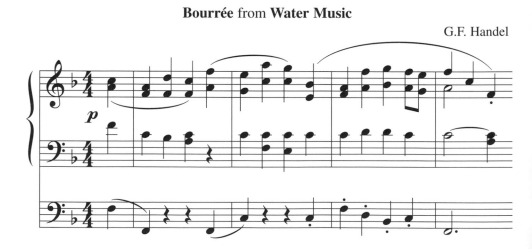

ORCHESTRAL SCORE can consist of many staves, as each instrument has its separate staff. Instrument families are grouped together.

Brandenburg Concerto no. 4

J.S. Bach

2 2.   VOCAL music is often written for a combination of the four different voices—soprano, contralto (often shortened to "alto"), tenor, and bass. It can be written two ways: in SHORT SCORE or in OPEN SCORE.

2 3.   SHORT SCORE (also called compressed or condensed score) begins like piano score: two staves are joined on the left side by a system line preceded by a brace. However, in vocal music, bar lines do not run through and connect both staves, as they do in piano music.

In short score, the soprano and alto parts are written in the treble clef, while the tenor and bass parts are written in the bass clef. When two different musical parts are written on one staff, some of the rules of notation differ from those that apply to music having a single part on each staff.

- The STEMS of the upper voice on each staff (i.e., soprano and tenor) go up, while those of the lower voice on each staff (i.e., alto and bass) go down, in this way eliminating any confusion about which note is sung by which voice. When the same note is sung by two voices at the same time, it is given two stems, one up and one down. If two voices sing a whole note in unison, two notes placed close together must be used.

     Example:

- For a DOTTED NOTE in a space, the dot goes in the same space. For a dotted soprano or tenor note on a line, the dot goes in the space above. For a dotted alto or bass note on a line, the dot goes in the space below. Dotted unison notes require only *one* dot.

- SLURS and TIES in the soprano and tenor parts curve upward. Slurs and ties in the alto and bass parts curve downward.

- RESTS are placed higher or lower than usual on the staff or even outside the staff (use ledger lines for breve, whole, and half rests) to avoid collisions between the two parts on a staff.

2 4. In OPEN SCORE, each of the four voices is written on its own staff. The voices appear in order of range, from highest to lowest. All four staves are connected on the left with a system line and a bracket.

In an open score of vocal music, each of the four parts has separate bar lines. This allows the text to be written under each part. (Texts have been omitted from the exercises that follow.) Be sure that the bar lines are aligned vertically.

Stems, dots, ties, slurs, rests, and so on, are placed according to the rules presented in Chapter 1. Fermatas are placed above each of the four parts. The main tempo marking is written only above the top staff. Dynamics and tempo changes, such as *rit.* or *accel.*, are written above each of the four parts.

The old form of vocal open score had each voice written in its own clef. The version shown here is known as VOCAL SCORE WITH C CLEFS FOR THE ALTO AND TENOR PARTS. Here is the excerpt above written in this form.

2 5. MODERN VOCAL SCORE does not use C clefs. The upper three voices are all written in the treble clef, but the tenor notes are written an octave higher than they sound. This method of writing is also known as novello score.

2 6. Music written for STRING QUARTET also has four staves. The instrumentation is: first violin, second violin, viola, and violoncello (often shortened to "cello"). The two violin parts are written in treble clefs. The usual clef for the viola part is the alto clef and the usual clef for the cello part is the bass clef. Notice that in string quartet score, the bar lines run through and connect all four staves.

2 EXERCISES

1. Write the following in short (condensed) score.

2.   Write the following passage in open score for string quartet.

3.   Write the following passage in short (condensed) score.

4. (a) Write the following passage in modern vocal score.

(b) Transpose the above passage into the key of E minor.

5.   (a) Write the following passage in open score, using C clefs for alto and tenor.

(b) Transpose the above passage up a major 3rd.

6.   (a) Write the following passage in modern vocal score.

       (b) Transpose the above passage into A minor.

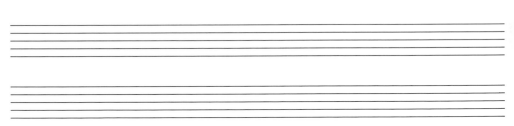

7.   Write the following passage in open score for string quartet.

8. Transpose the following passage down a minor 3rd, writing it in open score, using C clefs for alto and tenor.

CHAPTER 10

TERMS, SIGNS, AND ABBREVIATIONS

ITALIAN, FRENCH, AND GERMAN TERMS

The following are commonly used Italian terms and abbreviations grouped according to tempo, style, volume, etc.

1. **WORDS THAT REFER TO TEMPO**

P 1 2	SLOW	largo	very slow and broad
		larghetto	less slow than *largo*
		lento	slow
		adagio	slow (slower than *andante* but not as slow as *largo*)
P 1 2	MEDIUM	andante	rather slow, at a moderate, walking pace
		andantino	a little faster than *andante*
		moderato	moderate tempo
		allegretto	fairly quick, slightly slower than *allegro*
P 1 2	FAST	allegro	lively, fast
		presto	very fast
		prestissimo	as fast as possible
P 1 2	OTHERS	tempo	time; speed at which music is performed
1 2		con moto	with movement
		grave	extremely slow and solemn
		vivace	lively, brisk
2		comodo	at a comfortable, easy tempo

2. **WORDS THAT REFER TO VARIATIONS IN TEMPO**

P 1 2	a tempo	in time; return to the original tempo after an increase or decrease in tempo
	rallentando, rall.	slowing down gradually
	ritardando, rit.	slowing down gradually
	tempo primo, tempo I	return to the original tempo
1 2	accelerando, accel.	becoming quicker
	meno mosso	less movement, slower
	più mosso	more movement, quicker
	rubato	a flexible tempo, using slight variations of speed to enhance musical expression

2	allargando, allarg.	broadening, becoming slower
	l'istesso tempo	at the same tempo
	ritenuto, riten.	suddenly slower, held back
	stringendo, string.	pressing, becoming faster

3. WORDS THAT REFER TO VOLUME

P 1 2	pianissimo, **pp**	very soft
	piano, **p**	soft
	mezzo piano, **mp**	moderately soft
	mezzo forte, **mf**	moderately loud
	forte, **f**	loud
	fortissimo, **ff**	very loud

4. WORDS THAT REFER TO VARIATIONS IN VOLUME

P 1 2	crescendo, cresc.	becoming louder
	decrescendo, decresc.	becoming softer
	diminuendo, dim.	becoming softer
1 2	fortepiano, **fp**	loud, then suddenly soft
2	sforzando, sforzato, **sf** or **sfz**	a sudden, strong accent on a single note or chord

5. COMMON WORDS THAT REFER TO STYLE IN PLAYING

P 1 2	cantabile	in a singing style
	dolce	sweet
	grazioso	graceful
	legato	smooth
	maestoso	majestic
	marcato, marc.	marked, emphasized
	staccato	detached
1 2	animato	animated, spirited
	brillante	brilliant
	con brio	with vigor or vivacity
	con espressione	with expression
	espressivo, espress.	expressively
	leggiero	light
	tenuto	held
	tranquillo	tranquil
2	ad libitum, ad lib.	at the performer's liberty
	agitato	agitated, excited
	con fuoco	with fire
	con grazia	with grace
	dolente	doleful, sorrowful

2	giocoso	humorous, jocose
	grandioso	grand, grandiose
	largamente	broadly
	martellato	strongly accented, hammered
	mesto	sad, mournful
	morendo	dying, fading away
	pesante	weighty, with emphasis
	scherzando	playful
	semplice	simple
	sonore	sonorous
	sostenuto, sost.	sustained
	sotto voce	soft, subdued, under the breath
	strepitoso	boisterous, noisy
	vivo	lively

6. OTHER ITALIAN WORDS

P 1 2	con pedale, Ped.	with pedal
	da capo, D.C.	from the beginning
	dal segno, D.S.	from the sign 𝄋
	fine	end, close
	mano destra, M.D.	right hand
	mano sinistra, M.S.	left hand
	ottava, 8va	an octave

| 1 2 | loco | place; return to the written register |
| | tre corde | three strings; an indication in piano music to stop using the soft pedal |

2	arco	for stringed instruments: played with the bow
	attacca	do not pause between sections or movements
	con sordino	played with a mute
	pizzicato, pizz.	for stringed instruments: plucked with the fingers
	primo, prima	first; the upper part of a duet
	secondo, seconda	second; the lower part of a duet
	tacet	silence (used in orchestral parts)
	tutti	for the whole ensemble
	volta subito, v.s.	turn the page quickly

7. WORDS USED IN CONJUNCTION WITH OTHER WORDS

1 2	alla, all'	in the style of
	assai	very
	ben, bene	well
	col, coll', colla, colle	with the
	con	with

1 2	e, ed	and
	ma	but
	meno	less
	molto	much, very
	non	not
	non troppo	not too much
	più	more
	poco	little
	poco a poco	little by little
	quasi	almost, as if
	sempre	always, continuously
	senza	without
	troppo	too much
2	simile	like; continue in the same manner as has just been indicated
	subito, sub.	suddenly
	volta	time (as in *prima volta, seconda volta*)

2 8. FRENCH TERMS

	léger	light, lightly
	lentement	slowly
	modéré	at a moderate tempo
	mouvement	tempo; motion
	vite	fast

2 9. GERMAN TERMS

	bewegt	moving
	langsam	slow, slowly
	mässig	moderate, moderately
	mit Ausdruck	with expression
	schnell	fast
	sehr	very

SIGNS AND ABBREVIATIONS

Some of the following have already appeared in the section on Italian terms. They are repeated here in order to make the list of signs and abbreviations as complete as possible.

10. **TEMPO AND VARIATIONS IN TEMPO**

P 1 2   rall. (rallentando)   slowing down gradually
              rit. (ritardando)   slowing down gradually
              tempo I, tempo primo   return to the original tempo

1 2   accel. (accelerando)   becoming quicker

2   allarg. (allargando)   broadening, becoming slower
              riten. (ritenuto)   suddenly slower, held back
              string. (stringendo)   pressing, becoming faster

11. **VOLUME AND VARIATIONS IN VOLUME**

P 1 2   *pp* (pianissimo)   very soft
              p (piano)   soft
              mp (mezzo piano)   moderately soft
              mf (mezzo forte)   moderately loud
              f (forte)   loud
              ff (fortissimo)   very loud
              $<$ becoming louder
              cresc. (crescendo)   becoming louder
              $>$ becoming softer
              decresc. (decrescendo)   becoming softer
              dim. (diminuendo)   becoming softer

Opt.   *ppp* (piano possibile)   as soft as possible
              fff (forte possibile)   as loud as possible

12. **STYLE**

1 2   espress. (espressivo)   expressively

2   ad lib. (ad libitum)   at the performer's liberty
              sost. (sostenuto)   sustained

13. ACCENTS

P 1 2   > ♩ or ♩̂   accent; a stressed note

     marc. (marcato)   marked or emphasized

1 2   *fp* (fortepiano)   loud, then immediately soft

2   *sf* or *sfz* (sforzando)   a sudden, strong accent on a single note or chord

Opt.   ♩̱ or ♩̄   a slight accent; held for its full time value

14. REPEATS

P 1 2   𝄇   repeat from the previous section from   𝄆
     or from the beginning

     D.C. (da capo)   from the beginning

     D.S. (dal segno)   from the sign 𝄋

     fine   end, close; often used after D.C. or D.S. to indicate where the end is

Opt. |1st| |2nd| the passage is to be repeated, but with the ending changed the second time

15. REPEATED GROUPS

Opt.   bis   twice

     is played like this

     / ⁒ and // are all signs used to indicate the repetition of a measure, or a figure within a measure

     is played like this

     is played like this

     is played like this

16. REPEATED NOTES

Opt.

to be played as repeated eighth notes, like this

to be played as repeated sixteenth notes, like this

to be divided into four notes of equal value, and repeated

to be repeated like this

in as many sixteenth notes as are equal to a half note

tremolo – repeat the note as rapidly as possible within the time value of the note

17. DEGREES OF STACCATO

"Staccato" means short or detached. A staccato note can be expressed in three different ways.

P 1 2

1. staccato – the note is held for about half its value, like this

Opt.

2. staccatissimo – very short, held for about a quarter of its value, like this

3. mezzo staccato – slightly detached, like this

If a group of notes is to be played mezzo staccato, a slur accompanies the dots.

18. DIFFERENT FORMS OF

P 1 2

1. A TIE joins two notes of the same pitch.

2. A SLUR joins two or more notes of different pitch. The notes within the slur all belong to one phrase, and are to be played in a *legato* style.

3. A SLUR in vocal music marks the notes sung to one syllable.

Faith of our   fa – thers,   liv – ing   still

P 1 2   4.   A BOW MARK   in music for strings, all the notes within the slur are to
                                      be played with one bow.

19.   **MISCELLANEOUS**

P 1 2   ⌢   fermata—indicates a pause. The note (or rest) is to be held longer than
                        its normal value.

M.D.   (mano destra) or RH means right hand

M.S.   (mano sinistra) or LH means left hand

8va-------- when placed above notes, play them an octave higher

8va-------- when placed below notes, play them an octave lower

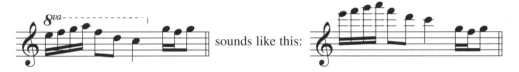

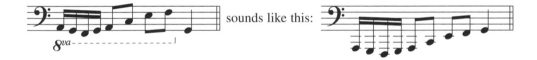

1 2   Sometimes "*loco*" is used to show where the music returns to its normal position.

Opt.   Con *8va* means to play the notes in octaves.

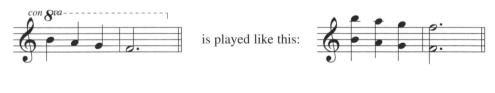

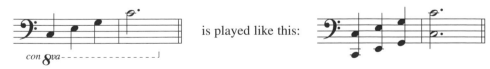

⊓ and V are bow marks for string music:

V means an up bow—your arm moves *towards* your body

⊓ means a down bow—your arm moves *away* from your body

264

P 1 2	𝄢. ❋	put down the damper pedal at 𝄢. and let it up at ❋
		Another way of showing this is └────∧────┘
1 2	M.M.	Maelzel's Metronome. An instrument used for beating time. At the beginning of a piece, the composer indicates the kind of note which is to get one beat, and the number of times that the metronome is to tick each minute. Thus, MM ♩ =96 means that the piece is to be played at the speed of 96 quarter notes per minute.
Opt.	⸲ (a comma)	a slight break in the flow of the music, or a breath mark
	tr〜〜	a trill—a rapid alternation of the note with the note above it
	(chord)	to be played as an arpeggio—that is, not sounded together as a solid chord, but following each other quickly, starting with the bottom note
	(glissando)	a glissando—it means to draw the finger quickly up (or down) a series of adjacent notes
	6 (rest)	multi-measure rest—there is to be a period of silence for 6 measures

CHAPTER 11

DICTIONARY OF TERMS AND FORMS

The following table is a comprehensive list of musical terms, and is intended to serve only as a brief dictionary. It includes all the terms in Chapter 10, as well as many more that are in common usage.

A

a	for, at, in, etc.
a cappella	unaccompanied choral music
a capriccio	in a capricious or humorous style
a piacere	at the performer's liberty
accelerando	becoming quicker
adagio	slow (slower than *andante* but not as slow as *largo*)
ad libitum	at the performer's liberty
affabile	in a pleasing manner
affettuoso	affectionate, with tender warmth
affrettando	hurrying
agitato	agitated, excited
al fine	to the end
al, alla, alle, all'	to the, in the style of
alla breve	make the half note the beat
allargando	broadening, becoming slower
alla Tedesca	in the German style
allegretto	fairly fast, slightly slower than *allegro*
allegro	lively, fast
allegro assai	very quick
allegro giusto	quick, with exactness
allegro moderato	moderately quick
amabile	sweet, loveable
amore	tenderness and affection
amoroso	loving
andante	rather slow, at a moderate, walking pace
andantino	a little faster than *andante*
andare	go on
Anglaise	in the English style
anima (con anima)	spirit (with spirit)
animato	animated, spirited
anime	lively, spirited
animoso	in a lively manner
antico	ancient
a piacere	at pleasure
a poco	by degrees, gradually
a poco a poco	little by little
appassionato	impassioned
appenato	grieved, distressed
appoggiato	leaning upon, drawn out
arco, arcato	for stringed instruments: played with the bow
ardente	with fire, vehemently
ardore	with love and warmth
arioso	in the style of an air

arpeggio	playing the notes of a chord successively instead of simultaneously (harp style)
assai	very, extremely
assai più	much more
a tempo	in time, that is, return to the original tempo after an increase or decrease in tempo
attacca	do not pause between sections or movements

B

barocco	baroque, eccentric, bizarre
bassa	low, deep
basso	the bass part, the lowest male voice
basso continuo	a bass that is figured to indicate the harmony
ben, bene	well, good
bene placito	at will, at pleasure
ben marcato	well marked or accented
bewegt (German)	moving
binary	two-fold
binary form	a form of two divisions or sections
bis twice	(the passage is to be repeated)
bravura	spirit, skill
breve	a double whole note ‖O‖ equal to two semi-breves or whole notes
brillante	brilliant, bright, sparkling
brio	vigor, vivacity, spirit
buffa, buffo	comic, humorous
burlando	in a playful manner

C

cadenza	cadence; the elaboration (originally improvised) of the (final) cadence chords by a soloist
calando	gradually decreasing the time and tone
calcando	hurrying the time
calmato	tranquility
caloroso	warmth, animation
cantabile	in a singing style
cantando	in a singing style
canto	song, melody
capo	the beginning, the top
cappella	a chapel
carezzando	in a tender manner
carità	compassion, feeling
celere	quick, rapid
cembalo	a harpsichord
coda	a section of a composition added on to the end, as a conclusion
col, coll', colla, colle	with the
colla voce	with the voice
coll'arco	with the bow
coloratura	ornamental passage in vocal music
come	as, like
come prima	as before
comodo	at a comfortable, easy tempo; quietly, easily
compiacevole	agreeable
con	with

concento	harmony of voices and instruments
con sordini	in strings, with mutes; in piano, with dampers, that is the damper pedal is not to be used
continuo	without cessation
contralto	the deepest female voice
crescendo	becoming louder

D

da	by, from, for, etc.
da capo	from the beginning; a sign at the end of a movement indicating that the player must return to the beginning
da capo al fine	return to the beginning and play to the word "fine"
dal, dalle, dalla	from the, by the, etc.
dal segno	repeat from the sign 𝄋
debile	weak, feeble
deciso	in a bold manner, with decision
decrescendo	becoming softer
delicato	delicately
destra	the right hand
devoto	religious
di	of, with, from, etc.
difficile	difficult
dignità	dignity, grandeur
diminuendo	becoming softer
di molto	very much
discreto	discreetly
di sopra	above
disperato	with desperation
divisi	separated (half the players play the upper notes, and the others play the lower notes)
dolce	sweet
dolente	doleful, sorrowful
dolore	sorrow, grief
doloroso	sorrowfully
dopo	after
doppio movimento	double the preceding speed
drammatico	dramatic
dritta, dritto	the right hand
due corde	two strings; the una corda pedal is to be put half-way down
duo	two, in two parts, duet
duolo	sorrow, sadness
duro	harsh, rude

E

e, ed.	and
effetto	the effect of music on an audience
egualmente	evenly, alike
elegante, eleganza	graceful, elegant
elegiaco	plaintive
emozione	agitation
energico	forcibly
enfatico	emphatic
entre'acte	music played between acts of a drama
epico	heroic

equabilmente	evenly
espressione	expression
espressivo	expressively
estinto	becoming extinct
estremamente	extremely

F

facile	light, easy
facilemente	easily, without strain
fantastico	whimsical
fastoso	proudly, stately
ferma	resolute, steady
fermata	a pause or hold
fermato	firmly, resolutely
feroce	fierce, ferocious
fervente	ardent
fervido	vehement
festivo, festoso	merry, festive
fiacco	feeble, weak
fieramente	boldly
fine	the end, close
finement	delicately
flebile	sad, mournful
forte	loud
forte-piano	loud, then suddenly soft
forte possibile	as loud as possible
fortissimo	very loud
forza	force, strength
forzando, forzato	forced, usually on one note or chord
freddezza	coldness
fretta	increasing the time
funerale	mournful
fuoco	fire, passion
furioso	furiously
furore	fury, rage

G

gaio	with cheerfulness
galante	boldly, gallantly
garbato	graceful
garbo	grace, elegance
generoso	in a dignified manner
gentile	pleasing, elegant
giocando	cheerful, merry
giocoso	humorously, jocose
giubilazione	jubilant
giusto (con giusto)	just, right, proper (with proper taste)
giustezza	precision
glissando	in a gliding manner, slurred
gradevole	pleasant, agreeable
gradualmente	gradually, by degrees
grandioso	grand, majestic
grave	extremely slow and solemn

	grazia	grace
	grazioso	in a graceful style
	grosso	full, great
	grottesco	grotesque
	gusto	taste, expression
I	I, il	the
	il più	the most
	im	in the
	imitando	imitating
	impaziente	impatient, hurried
	imperioso	pompous
	impetuoso	vehement, in an energetic manner
	imponente	haughtily
	in	in, in the
	incalzando	with growing warmth
	inconsolato	in a mournful style
	inquieto	restless, uneasy
	instantemente	urgently
	intimo	intimate, inward
	intrepidamente	boldly
	irato	angrily
	ironico	ironical
	irresoluto	wavering
	istesso	the same
	istesso tempo	the same time
J	jubiloso	exulting
L	la	the
	lacrimoso	weeping, tearful
	lamentando	mourning
	lamentoso	mournful
	langsam (German)	slow, slowly
	languendo, languido	feeble, languishing
	largamente	broadly
	larghetto	less slow than *largo*
	largo	very slow and broad
	legatissimo	exceedingly smooth
	legato	smooth
	léger (French)	light, lightly
	leggiero	light
	lentando	with increased slowness
	lentement (French)	slowly
	lento	slow
	lestamente	quickly, lively
	lesto	lively quick
	libero	free, unrestrained
	liscio	simple, smooth
	l'istesso	the same
	loco	place; return to the written register after playing an octave higher or lower

lontano	distant, a great way off
lugubre	sad, mournful
lunga pausa	a long pause
lusingando	alluring, flattering
luttuoso	sorrowful

M

ma	but
maestoso	majestic
maggiore	the major key
main droite (French)	right hand
main gauche (French)	left hand
mancando	dying away
mässig (German)	moderate, moderately
maniera	manner, style
mano	the hand
mano destra	the right hand
mano sinistra	the left hand
marcando, marcato	marked, emphasized
martellato	strongly accented, hammered
marziale	in the style of a march
meno	less
mesto, mestoso	sad, mournful
mezza, mezzo	moderately, medium, half
mezzo soprano	a female voice lower than a soprano but higher than a contralto
minacciando	menacing
misterioso	in a mysterious manner
misurato	in strict, measured time
mit Ausdruck (German)	with expression
mobile	changeable
moderato	at a moderate tempo
modéré (French)	at a moderate tempo
molto	much, very, very much, a great deal
morendo	dying, fading away
mormoroso	with a gentle, murmuring sound
mosso	movement, motion
moto (con moto)	movement, motion (rather quick)
moto perpetuo	perpetual motion
mouvement (French)	tempo, motion
movimento	impulse, the time of a piece

N

negligente	unconstrained, careless
nel, nella, nell'	in the, at the
nobile	noble, grand
nobilimente	nobly
non	not, no

O

obbligato	indispensable, must not be omitted
opus	work, composition
ossia	otherwise, or else
ostinato	continuous, unceasing
ottava	an octave, an eighth
ottava alta	the octave higher
ottava bassa	the octave lower

P

parlando, parlante	accented; in a recitative or speaking style
passionato, passionatamente	impassioned, passionate
passione	passion
patetica	pathetic
pateticamente	pathetically
pausa	a pause
paventato	fearful
pedale	pedal (con pedale—with pedal)
per	for, by, from, etc.
perdendosi	gradually decreasing in time and tone, dying away and becoming slower
pesante	weighty, with emphasis
piacere	pleasure, fancy
piacevole	pleasing, agreeable
piangevole	mournful, plaintively
pianissimo	very soft
piano	soft
piena, pieno	full
pieta	pity
pictoso	tenderly, pitifully
più	more
più mosso, più moto	more motion
pizzicato	for stringed instruments: plucked with the fingers
placidamente	peacefully
placido	calm, tranquil
pochettino, pochetto	very little
poco	little
poco a poco	little by little
poi	then, afterwards
poi a poi	by degrees
pomposo	pompous
ponderoso	massively, heavily
ponticello	the bridge of a stringed instrument
possibile	possible
precipitato	hurriedly
precipitando	hurrying
precisione	exactness
preciso	precise, exact
prestissimo	as fast as possible
presto	very fast
primo, prima	first; the upper part of a duet
prima volta	the first time

Q

quasi	almost; as if; in the manner of
quieto	quick, calm, serene

R

rallentando	slowing down gradually
rapidamente, rapido	rapidly
rattenuto	holding back
religioso	solemnly, in a devout manner
replica	repeat
replicazione	repetition
rigore	strictness (con rigore—in strict time)

rinforzando	reinforced, strengthening the tone
ripetizione	repetition
risoluto	bold, resolved, resolutely
ritardando	gradually getting slower
ritenuto	suddenly slower, held back
rubato	a flexible tempo, using slight variations of speed to enhance musical expression
rustico	rural, rustic

S

scherzando	playful, lively
schnell (German)	fast
sciolto	freedom, ease
se	if, in case, as
secco	dry, staccato
secondo, seconda	second; the lower part of a duet
segno (dal segno)	a sign (repeat from the sign)
segue	now follows, go on with what follows
sehr (German)	very
semplice	simple
sempre	always, continuously
sentimento	feeling, delicate expression
senza	without
serioso	serious
sforzando	strongly accented
simile	like; continue in the same manner as has just been indicated
slargando	broadening
slentando	getting slower
smorzando	toning down to extinction
soave	gentle, soft, suave
soavità	sweetness, gentleness
solenne	solemn
solennellement	solemnly
solo	a composition for a single voice or instrument, alone
sonore	sonorous, harmonious
sordamente	softly, gently
sordino	a mute
sostenuto	sustained
sotto voce	softly, sublevel, under the breath
spianato	smooth, even
spiccato	separated, detached; a loose bouncing movement in the middle of the bow
spirito	spirit, life
stabile	firm
staccato	detached
stanchezza	weariness
stentando	heavy and retarding
stentato	forced, loud
stesso	the same
strascinato	dragged along
strepitoso	boisterous, noisy
stringendo	pressing, becoming faster
su	above, upon
subito	suddenly

	sul, sull, sulla	on, upon the, near
	sussurando	whispering, murmuring
	svelto	quick, nimble
T	tacet	be silent
	tanto	so much, as much
	tardamente	slowly
	Tedesca	German
	tema	theme or subject
	tempo	time; speed at which music is performed
	tempo comodo	easily, without haste
	tempo giusto	in strict time, in exact time
	tempo ordinario	in moderate time, at an ordinary speed
	tempo primo	return to the original time
	tempo rubato	robbed or irregular time
	teneramente	tenderly
	tenuto	held
	tessitura	the average range of a vocal part
	timoroso	with hesitation
	tosto	swift, rapid
	tranquillo	tranquil
	trascinando	dragging the time
	tre	three
	tre corde	three strings; an indication in piano music to stop using the soft pedal
	tremolo	rapid repetition of a note
	trionfale	triumphal
	tristezza	sadness, heaviness
	troppo	too much (non troppo—not too much)
	tutta, tutti	all, for the whole ensemble
U	uguale	equal, similar
	un, una, uno	a, an, one
	una corda	one string; a direction in piano music to use the soft pedal
V	va	go on
	vaccilando	irregular in time
	vago	rambling, uncertain as to time or expression
	veloce	swiftly, with velocity
	velocissimo	with extreme rapidity
	vibrato	a slight varying of pitch produced by the rapid movement of the left hand on a stringed instrument
	vigoroso	bold, energetic, vigorous
	violento	boisterous, vehement
	vitemente (French)	briskly
	vite (French)	fast
	vivace	lively, brisk
	vivo	lively
	volta	time
	volta prima	first time
	volta seconda	the second time
	volti	turn over
	volti subito	turn the page over quickly

FORMS

The following is a list of some of the forms of compositions (with a brief definition of each) you are likely to encounter during early and intermediate years of music study.

AIR (AYRE) – a melodious composition used in some Baroque suites, which was designed to accompany dancing; not one of the standard dance forms such as the Gavotte or the Minuet.

ALLEMANDE – the first of the dances in the Baroque suite, written in duple time and played at a moderate tempo.

ANGLAISE – an English country dance, sometimes part of the suite, in quick duple time, always starting on a strong beat.

ARABESQUE – a light and graceful piece with florid ornamentation in the melody.

ARIA – a melodic composition for solo voice with accompaniment, or a song-like composition written in ABA form.

ARIETTA – a small aria in binary form, that is, not having the middle section of the aria.

BAGATELLE – literally, a "trifle" – a short unpretentious composition.

BALLADE – a piece of a romantic type, usually in ABA form, combining dramatic and lyrical characteristics.

BARCAROLLE – a lyrical boat song usually in moderate $\frac{6}{8}$ or $\frac{12}{8}$ time, and ABA form, supposed to be derived from the songs of the Venetian gondoliers.

BERCEUSE – a lullaby, a quiet piece generally in moderate $\frac{6}{8}$ time, with a rocking movement in the accompaniment.

BOLERO – a quick Spanish dance in $\frac{3}{4}$ time with accompaniment of castanets.

BOURRÉE – a French or Spanish dance, usually in quick duple time, starting on an upbeat; often found in Baroque suites.

CANON – a composition in which each part has exactly the same melody throughout the piece, starting at different points. The strictest form of imitation.

CANTATA – a work for chorus and soloists with orchestral accompaniment.

CANZONET – a little song or piece with passages of imitation, something like a madrigal.

CAPRICCIO (CAPRICE) – a piece of fight and humorous style, usually in irregular form.

CHACONNE – a slow dance, very similar to a Passacaglia, probably originally from Spain. Usually in a major key, in $\frac{3}{4}$ time, with a ground bass and generally in the form of variations.

CHORALE – a German Protestant hymn tune, upon which larger compositions such as the choral prelude were based.

CONCERTO – a composition for one or more solo instruments with orchestral accompaniment, usually written in three movements.

COURANTE (CORRENTE) – an old dance in AB form, literally meaning "running." Usually in triple time, and the second of the standard movements of the suite. The Italian Corrente is much quicker than the more refined French Courante, which frequently shifted from $\frac{3}{2}$ to $\frac{6}{4}$ time.

ÉCOSSAISE – originally a slow dance in $\frac{3}{4}$ time, allegedly of Scottish origin but not at all similar to the Scottish dance music, such as the reel. Later, it became livelier and was written in duple time.

ENTRÉE – an introduction; a march-like piece played during the entrance of a dancing group, or played before a ballet. Usually in $\frac{4}{4}$ time.

ÉTUDE – a study written for the purpose of practicing and developing facility in a special problem of technique, or for displaying the technical skill of the performer.

FANTASIA – a movement free in spirit and form, rather like an improvisation.

FUGUE – a form of imitative counterpoint written for two or more voices, brought to its highest point of refinement by J.S. Bach. It is based on a short theme or subject, stated at the beginning by one voice, and brought in by each of the others in turn.

GAVOTTE – an old French dance form, stately and dignified, in duple time, beginning on the weak half of the measure; sometimes found in Baroque suites. It was often followed by another Gavotte or a Musette, and then repeated.

GIGUE (JIG) – a lively dance in $\frac{6}{8}$ or $\frac{12}{8}$ time, usually the final movement of a suite. It is contrapuntal in style with the second half frequently using the inverted subject.

HOPAK – a lively Russian dance in simple duple time.

HORNPIPE – a very lively English dance, first written in triple time but later in quadruple time. Now usually associated with sailors, but this apparently has no historical basis.

IMPROMPTU – a piece that suggests improvisation, that has a feeling of informality. First used in the early 19th century.

INTERMEZZO – an interlude; a piece designed originally to be performed between the acts of a play or opera.

INTRATA (INTRADA) – the name given to an opening piece of march-like character. The Italian equivalent of an Entrée or Prelude.

INVENTION – a short contrapuntal piece for two or three voices, in imitative style.

LÄNDLER – a popular German or Austrian dance in $\frac{3}{4}$ or $\frac{3}{8}$ time, thought to be the true origin of the waltz. It is very like a waltz, though slower.

LOURÉ – a slow French dance in $\frac{6}{4}$ time, sometimes found in the Baroque Suite. Its chief characteristic is the rhythm ♩ ♩ ♩ ♩, often used.

MADRIGAL – a composition for unaccompanied voices. It originated in Italy in the 15th century, and was written for two to eight voices.

MARCH – a piece written in simple duple or quadruple time, strongly accented, used for accompanying marching (usually of soldiers).

MAZURKA – a Polish national dance in moderate $\frac{3}{4}$ time, with strong accents on the third beat, and sometimes on the second.

MINUET (MENUET) – a French dance in triple time, usually followed by a TRIO and then repeated. The early minuets were rather dignified and graceful, but the later ones became faster and lighter in character.

MUSETTE – a short French dance-tune of pastoral character, with a drone bass, originally played on a bagpipe. Found in some suites, usually following a Gavotte.

NOCTURNE – literally "night piece." A romantic, dreamy piece for piano, written with a melody over a broken-chord accompaniment.

OPERA – a drama set to music for soloists, chorus, and orchestra.

ORATORIO – a sacred work for soloists, chorus, and orchestra, something like an opera but performed without action, costumes or scenery.

OVERTURE – a prelude to an opera, play, or oratorio.

PARTITA – a word meaning either a suite or a set of variations.

PASSACAGLIA – a chaconne with a ground bass in slow triple time, and always in a minor key.

PASSEPIED – a spirited French dance in $\frac{3}{8}$ or $\frac{6}{8}$ time, sometimes used in the Baroque suite.

PASTORALE – a piece written to imitate the music of shepherds, usually in moderate $\frac{6}{8}$ or $\frac{12}{8}$ time; a tender flowing melody, somewhat suggestive of a Musette.

PAVANE – a slow solemn dance in duple (or sometimes triple) time, of Spanish origin; generally in three sections, each one repeated.

POLONAISE (POLACCA) – a Polish dance in moderate $\frac{3}{4}$ time. The phrases end on the third beat of the measure, and there are many repetitions of short motives. It is not a folk dance, but originated from court ceremonies.

PRELUDE – a piece designed to be played as an introduction, but also an independent short romantic piece in an improvised manner.

REQUIEM – a Mass for the Dead, usually set to music for solo voices, chorus, and orchestra.

RHAPSODY – a free fantasy, usually of heroic or national character, and often brilliant in style.

RHUMBA (RUMBA) – a Cuban dance with complex rhythm, much syncopation, and repetition of an eight-measure theme.

RIGAUDON (English: RIGADOON) – a 17th century Provençal dance in lively duple or quadruple time. Something like a Bourrée, with the phrases beginning on the last quarter of the measure.

ROMANCE – a piece that is song-like, sentimental, and tender in character.

RONDO (French: RONDEAU) – a piece in which the main theme keeps recurring with different episodes between – ABACA. A more modern form is extended to ABACABA coda.

RONDINO – a small or easy rondo.

SARABANDE – a dignified dance, probably originally from Spain. In $\frac{3}{4}$ or $\frac{3}{2}$ time, usually starting on the first beat. It moves along at a steady pace, with an accent or a prolonged note on the second beat. It is in AB form, with the phrases ending on the second beat. Commonly found in Baroque suites.

SCHERZO (Italian meaning "joke") – a piece in $\frac{3}{4}$ time which is sometimes playful and joking, but also can be moody, gloomy and dramatic, such as those of Chopin.

SCHERZINO – a little scherzo.

SCHOTTISCHE – a round dance in $\frac{2}{4}$ time, something like a slow Polka, known in England as the German polka.

SERENADE – French for "evening music"—originally a love song sung under the window of a lady, by her lover; now an instrumental piece of similar character.

SICILIANO – a soft, slow peasant dance in $\frac{6}{8}$ or $\frac{12}{8}$ time, often in a minor key. Rather similar to a Pastorale, usually in ABA form. It usually has a melody in dotted rhythms, with a broken-chord accompaniment.

SOLFEGGIETTO – an Italian word meaning "little study."

SONATA – a work consisting of three or four independent pieces called movements, each of which follows certain forms and characteristics, written for one or two instruments. Similar works for three instruments are called TRIOS, for four instruments are called QUARTETS, and for orchestra are called SYMPHONIES.

SONATINA – a small, easier sonata with fewer and short movements.

SUITE – a group of pieces consisting (in the classical form) entirely of dance forms, and all in the same key. The basic movements included were the Allemande, Courante, Sarabande, Gigue, and then usually one or more others such as the Gavotte, Minuet, Bourrée, Passepied, etc. The suite was often preceded by a Prelude.

SYMPHONY – a composition for orchestra, similar to a sonata, but on a larger scale.

TARANTELLA – a wild Italian dance in $\frac{3}{8}$ or $\frac{6}{8}$ time, which was supposed to cure the poisonous bite of the spider called the tarantula. It frequently alternated modes, and increased in frenzy towards the end.

TOCCATA (Latin meaning "touch") – a virtuoso piece composed to display the technical skill of the player, usually with full chords, arpeggios, and running passages, in a free fantasy style.

TOCCATINA – a small, short toccata; sometimes used as an opening to a suite.

VARIATIONS (or AIR WITH VARIATIONS) – a musical form where the main theme is stated, and then subjected many times to a number of changes without entirely losing sight of its identity.

WALTZ – a dance in triple time which probably originated from the German Ländler; still a very popular form.

CHAPTER 12

ANALYSIS QUESTIONS AND TEST PAPERS

PRELIMINARY ANALYSIS

Analyse the following music excerpt by answering the questions below.

Piano Sonata, Hob. XVI: G1
Finale

1. Name the composer of this piece. _____

2. Add the correct time signature directly on the music.

3. On which beat does this piece begin? _____

4. Explain the meaning of *presto*. _____

5. Name the key of this piece. _____

6. Find and circle one example of a diatonic semitone. Label it DS.

7. For the passage at letter **A**:

   a) Name the *harmonic* interval between the notes. _____

   b) Name the technical degree (tonic, supertonic, or dominant) on which this passage begins, and the technical degree on which it ends.

      begins on: _____   ends on: _____

8. Name the interval at letter **B**. _____

9. Explain the sign at letter **C**. _____

   _____

GRADE ONE ANALYSIS

Analyse the following music excerpt by answering the questions below.

Piano Sonata, K 545
2nd movement

W. A. Mozart
(1756–1791)

1. Add the correct time signature directly on the music.

2. Explain the meaning of *andante*. _____

3. Name the key of this piece. _____

4. Name the triad at letter **A**.

    root: _____   position: _____   quality: _____

5. Name the triad at letter **B**.

    root: _____   position: _____   quality: _____

6. Name the interval at letter **C**. _____

7. Name the interval at letter **D**. _____

8. Name the triad at letter **E**.

    root: _____   position: _____   quality: _____

9. Name the triad at letter **F**.

    root: _____   position: _____   quality: _____

10. Name the harmonic interval on beat 2 of m. 8 of the left-hand part.

    _____

GRADE TWO ANALYSIS

Analyse the following music excerpt by answering the questions below.

Bagatelle, op. 119, no. 1

L. van Beethoven
(1770–1827)

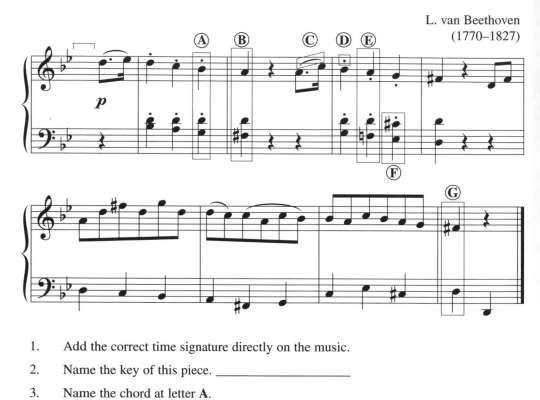

1. Add the correct time signature directly on the music.

2. Name the key of this piece. _____

3. Name the chord at letter **A**.

    root: _____   position: _____   quality: _____

4. Name the chord at letter **B**.

    root: _____   position: _____   quality: _____

5. Name and explain the sign at letter **C**. _____

    _____

6. Name and explain the sign at letter **D**. _____

    _____

7. Name the chord at letter **E**.

    root: _____   position: _____   quality: _____

8. a) Name the *harmonic* interval at letter **F**. _____

    b) Find and circle the *inversion* of this interval in melodic form.

9. Name the interval at letter **G**. _____

Marks **PRELIMINARY TEST PAPER**

(10) 1. a) Write the following as half notes in the bass clef.

A   E♭   F♯   B   D♭

b) Name the following notes.

____   ____   ____   ____   ____

(10) 2. a) Write a whole tone above each of the following notes.

b) Write a chromatic semitone below each of the following notes.

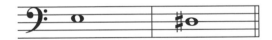

(10) 3. Write the following scales, ascending and descending, using whole notes.

a) E major in the treble clef, using accidentals
b) A♭ major in the bass clef, using a key signature
c) F♯ minor, natural form, in the bass clef, using a key signature
d) G minor, harmonic form, in the bass clef, using accidentals
e) C minor, melodic form, in the treble clef, using a key signature

a)

282

b)

c)

d)

e)

(10) 4. Write the following notes in the bass clef, using accidentals.

    a) the tonic of E minor
    b) the subdominant of F major
    c) the dominant of B minor
    d) the tonic of A♭ major
    e) the dominant of F♯ minor

a)   b)   c)   d)   e)

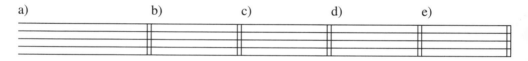

(10) 5. a) Write the following intervals above the given notes.

    per 4   maj 7   min 6   per 5   maj 2

    b) Name the following intervals.

283

(10) 6. Write the following triads in the treble clef, using key signatures.

     a) the subdominant triad of A major
     b) the dominant triad of C♯ minor harmonic
     c) the tonic triad of B♭ major
     d) the dominant triad of E♭ major
     e) the subdominant triad of D minor harmonic

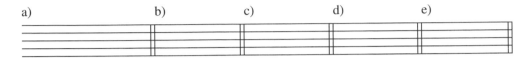

(10) 7. Add rests below the brackets to complete the following measures.

(10) 8. a) Name the key of the following melody. Transpose it down one octave into the bass clef.

key:_____

b) Name the key of the following melody. Transpose it up one octave into the treble clef.

key:_____

(10) 9. a) Explain the following terms.

lento   _____

decrescendo   _____

mano sinistra _____

allegretto   _____

da capo   _____

b) Draw the following signs on the given notes.

tie   fermata   staccato   slur   accent

(10) 10. a) Analyse the following melody by answering the questions below.

- Name its key.
- Add the correct time signature.
- Circle and label the subdominant note.
- Circle and label the tonic triad.
- Circle and label the dominant triad.

key:_____

b) Analyse the following melody by answering the questions below.

- Name its key.
- Add the correct time signature.
- Circle and label the dominant note. (There are three examples.)
- Circle and label a diatonic semitone. (There are five examples.)
- Circle and label an interval of a minor 6th.

key:_____

286

Marks   **GRADE ONE TEST PAPER**

(10)   1.   a)   Write the following scales, ascending and descending, using the correct key
signature for each. Use whole notes.

Cb major in the treble clef

D# minor, melodic form, in the bass clef

chromatic scale on Bb in the treble clef

b)   Identify the following scale types.

(10)   2.   Write the following notes in the bass clef, using accidentals.

a) the supertonic of Ab major
b) the leading note of G# minor harmonic
c) the subdominant of F minor
d) the submediant of B major
e) the mediant of C minor

a)   b)   c)   d)   e)

(10) 3. a) Write the following intervals above the given notes.

         per 4   aug 6   min 3   maj 7   dim 5

      b) Invert the above intervals and name the inversions.

_____   _____   _____   _____   _____

(10) 4. Write the following triads in the treble clef, using key signatures.

      a) the supertonic triad of A major in root position
      b) the dominant triad of B♭ minor harmonic in first inversion
      c) the submediant triad of E♭ major in root position
      d) the tonic triad of C♯ minor in second inversion
      e) the subdominant triad of G minor harmonic in first inversion

a)   b)   c)   d)   e)

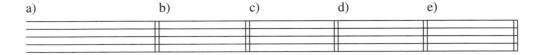

(10) 5. Write a two-measure example of each of the following cadences.

      a) perfect cadence in E major
      b) plagal cadence in D minor
      c) perfect cadence in B minor

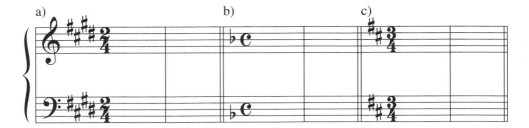

(10)   6.   Add rests below the brackets to complete the following measures.

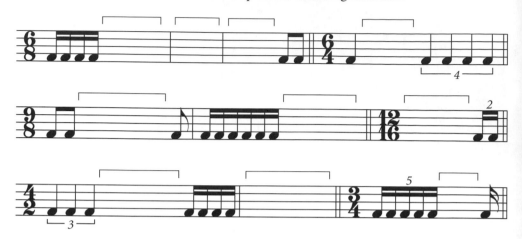

(10)   7.   For each of the following melodies, name the key and add the correct time signature.

(10) 8. a) Name the key of the following melody. Transpose it up an augmented 4th using the correct new key signature. Name the new key.

key:_____

_____

key:_____

b) Name the key of the following melody. Transpose it up a minor 3rd using the correct new key signature. Name the new key.

key:_____

_____

key:_____

(10) 9. a) Explain the following terms.

fortepiano_____

vivace_____

leggiero _____

grave _____

accelerando _____

b) Give the Italian word or phrase for each of the following.

but _____

with _____

little by little _____

more_____

not too much _____

290

(10)   10.   Analyse the following music excerpt by answering the questions below.

Kinder-Sonate, op. 118a, no. 1
1st movement

R. Schumann
(1810–1856)

a)   Name the composer of this piece. _____

b)   Name the key of this piece. _____

c)   How many times is the mediant note played in this piece? _____

d)   Explain the two signs at letter **A**. _____

e)   Explain the sign at letter **B**. _____

_____

f)   Name the interval at letter **C**. _____

g)   Name the interval at letter **D**. _____

h)   Name the triad at letter **E**.

   root: _____   position: _____   quality: _____

i)   Name the triad at letter **F**.

   root: _____   position: _____   quality: _____

j)   Name the triad at letter **G**.

   root: _____   position: _____   quality: _____

Marks   **GRADE TWO TEST PAPER**

(10)   1.   a)   Write the following scales and mode, ascending and descending, using the
                    correct key signature for each. Use whole notes.

C♯ major, from supertonic to supertonic, in the tenor clef

Eb minor, harmonic form, from dominant to dominant, in the bass clef

Dorian mode on Bb in the treble clef

b)   Write the following scale and mode, ascending and descending, using
        accidentals. Use whole notes.

G♯ minor, melodic form, from subdominant to subdominant, in the alto clef

Lydian mode on E in the bass clef

(10)   2.   a)   Write the following intervals below the given notes.

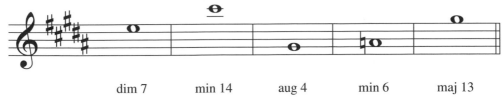

        dim 7   min 14   aug 4   min 6   maj 13

b)   Invert the above intervals in the bass clef, and name the inversions.

(10) 3. For each of the following triads, name:
   a) its root
   b) its position
   c) its quality

a) _____   _____   _____

b) _____   _____   _____

c) _____   _____   _____

   d) Name the scale that contains all of these triads._____

(10) 4. Write the following dominant 7th chords in the bass clef, using key signatures.

   a) the dominant 7th of A major in second inversion
   b) the dominant 7th of C minor in first inversion
   c) the dominant 7th of B major in third inversion
   d) the dominant 7th of D♯ minor in root position
   e) the dominant 7th of G minor in third inversion

a)   b)   c)   d)   e)

(10) 5. For the following:

   a) Name the key.
   b) Write a cadence at the end of the first phrase, and name the cadence.
   c) Write an answering phrase for the melody, ending with a perfect cadence.
      Draw the phrase mark for your answering phrase.

key: _____   _____

(10) 6. a) Add rests below the brackets to complete the following measures.

b) Add the correct time signature to each of the following.

(10) 7. a) Name the key of the following melody. Transpose it up an augmented 6th in the same clef, using the correct new key signature. Name the new key.

key:_____

key:_____

294

b) The following melody is written for clarinet in B♭. Name the key in which it is written. Transpose it to concert pitch, using the correct new key signature. Name the new key.

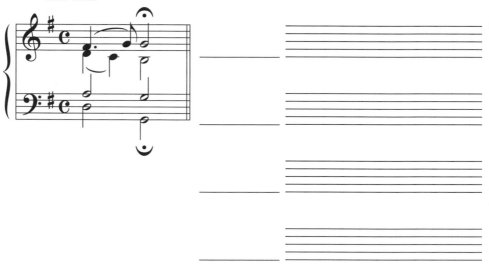

key:_____

key:_____

(10) 8. a) Rewrite the following passage in modern vocal score. Name the voice that sings each line.

b) The following passage is for string quartet. Name the instrument that plays each line. Rewrite the passage in short score.

(10)   9.   a)   Give an Italian term that has the same meaning as each of the following.

léger _____

vite _____

langsam _____

mässig _____

mit Ausdruck _____

b)   Define each of the following.

triad _____

_____

7th chord _____

_____

quartal chord _____

_____

polychord _____

_____

cluster _____

_____

(10) 10. Analyse the following music excerpt by answering the questions below.

Kinder-Sonate, op. 118a, no. 1
2nd movement

R. Schumann
(1810–1856)

a) In what year was the composer of this piece born? _____

b) Name the key of this piece. _____

c) Add the correct time signature directly on the music.

d) Name the interval at letter **A**. _____

e) Name the interval at letter **B**. _____

f) Name the chord at letter **C**.

    root: _____   position: _____   quality: _____

g) Name the chord at letter **D**.

    root: _____   position: _____   quality: _____

h) Name the chord at letter **E**.

    root: _____   position: _____   quality: _____

i) Name the the type of cadence at the end of this excerpt. _____

_____

j) Explain the meaning of *langsam*. _____

INDEX OF SUBJECTS

INDEX OF COMPOSERS AND SOURCES